A CLOSER WALK

DEVOTIONS BY STEVE TROXEL

VOLUME 3

A CLOSER WALK
Volume 3

Published by

God's Daily Word Ministries
http://www.gdwm.org

ISBN 0-9708531-6-5
Copyright © 2005
by
God's Daily Word Ministries.

Written by Steve Troxel

Cover Design by Al Mendenhall

Printed in Canada

CONTENTS

Days Of Our Youth 1

The Potter's Hand 3

What We've Seen And Heard..................... 5

Trusting In His Grace................................. 7

Guard Against The Yeast............................ 9

Spots Of A Leopard 11

This Last Day.. 13

The Mountain Of Faith 15

Listen As We Climb 17

Faith To Move Mountains......................... 19

In Spite Of Our Chains 21

Strain Toward The Vine............................. 23

Secure In His Presence.............................. 25

Misplaced Trust.. 27

Tools Of The Teacher................................. 29

Return To Give Thanks 31

Arise And Walk.. 33

Put It Into Practice 35

Stand Firm In The Gap 37

Never Lose Hope 39

These Are God's Battles............................. 41

Serve With Humility 43

Intended For Good 45

Never Forget... 47

Precious In His Sight 49

According To Your Will 51

Finish The Race 53

Who Taught Us To Walk 55

A Darkened Heart 57

An Unknown God 59

CONTENTS

Covenant Of Worship 61

A Broken Covenant 63

Continue To Seek 65

Guard The Good Deposit 67

How To Guard His Deposit 69

Free In The Fire 71

Be Prepared To Follow 73

Strong In His Grace 75

His Amazing Grace 77

Grace In Others 79

Spiritual Wisdom And Understanding 81

Nothing Too Hard 83

The Example Of Barnabas 85

Son Of Encouragement 87

Intentional Discipleship 89

God's Perfect Will 91

Actively Wait 93

By All Possible Means 95

Preach The Word 97

The Name Of Jesus 99

We Have Been Sent 101

God's Plumb Line 103

The Living Word 105

He Is Risen 107

Paid In Full 109

Dayenu - Jesus Is Enough 111

His Consuming Fire 113

Never Trade The Blessing 115

Stay Off The Roof 117

Two Become One Flesh 119

PREFACE

In August of 1996, as my wife and I were on the way to the hospital for the birth of our daughter, I sent a short email to a few friends and family. Unaware at the time, this was the beginning of God's Daily Word Ministries. The updates on my daughter's birth changed to short words of encouragement and scripture verses, and later grew to full devotionals.

Over the last several years, God has led thousands of people from all over the world to be a part of this growing ministry. As of this printing our email list consistst of over 25,000 individuals. This has been a wonderful journey of ever increasing faith and trust.

God has taught me that His main message is a continuous call to draw nearer and to love and trust Him more. This is His message when He first calls us to believe in Jesus for the for-giveness of sin and be restored to a relationship which has been broken for so long. It's also His message when we have journeyed with Him for a long while but are continuously subject to the pulls of the world.

This book is the third volume of what is intended to be a six volume set. The devotional messages in each of these books are written to give some instruction from God's Word as well as application and encouragement to draw nearer to God through trust, love and worship. These messages are for those who are seeking as well as those who have trusted Jesus for many years. I firmly believe that, no matter where we are in our relationship with God, we ALL are being called to A Closer Walk!

Steve Troxel

DAYS OF OUR YOUTH

All through the Old Testament, God called the people of Israel to worship Him as the One True God. He spoke through Moses, the priests, and the prophets; but the people continued to turn away. Even after the Babylonians invaded Jerusalem, God continued to call His Children to return to Him - to return with ALL their heart!

During the Babylonian captivity, God told Ezekiel to proclaim His Word to all the people of Israel. Ezekiel gave the people several illustrations of how far they had fallen, and how much sorrow their sin was causing for a loving Father. Through Ezekiel, God said the people of Israel were like a helpless newborn baby who had been thrown into an open field: "Then I passed by and saw you kicking about in your blood, and as you lay there in your blood I said to you, 'Live!'" (Ezekiel 16:6).

They had done nothing to deserve His favor, but were chosen to become a great nation, set apart and devoted to God. Without His grace, they would have been as lost as the newborn in the field - but God said "Live!" He picked them up, cleaned them off, loved them, and made them beautiful...but His Children forgot His love and abused His grace.

1

Ezekiel 16:15-16

"You trusted in your beauty and used your fame to become a prostitute. You lavished your favors on anyone who passed by and your beauty became his...such things should not happen."

The people of Israel forgot all God had done and gave their love to other gods (Spiritual prostitution). They used the grace of God for their own benefit and forgot their previous condition: "In all your detestable practices and your prostitution you did not remember the days of your youth, when you were naked and bare, kicking about in your blood" (Ezekiel 16:22).

God loves us so much...and it breaks His heart to see how we abuse His gifts. Without the saving grace of Jesus, each of us are as helpless as the newborn baby. Without Christ, we have no hope of survival: "But God demonstrates His own love for us in this: While we were still sinners, Christ died for us" (Romans 5:8). We were lost in our sin until God reached down, picked us up, and said "Live!" Thank You Lord!!

Let's remind ourselves of the miracle of Salvation! Though we have done nothing to deserve God's grace, He reaches down and gives us eternal life - cleansing us of our sins and making us beautiful in His sight. We who believe have been born into God's Family. Let's not abuse His gift by forgetting when we were helpless, "naked and bare." Let's give Him ALL our love and always remember the days of our youth.

THE POTTER'S HAND

About 2600 years ago, God taught the prophet Jeremiah what it meant to be a sovereign God. He taught that His plan WOULD be fulfilled - one way or the other. Either His children would submit to His gentle guidance, or He would bring discipline to teach them the need for obedience.

Although God has the ability to directly give us understanding, His usual method is to teach us through His Word and then allow us to see the application and gain wisdom through our experiences. In order to give a clear understanding of His sovereignty, God told Jeremiah to go to the potter's house and wait for His message.

Jeremiah 18:3-6

"So I went down to the potter's house, and I saw him working at the wheel. But the pot he was shaping from the clay was marred in his hands; so the potter formed it into another pot, shaping it as seemed best to him. Then the Word of the Lord came to me: 'Can I not do with you as this potter does?' declares the Lord. 'Like clay in the hand of the potter, so are you in My hand.'"

3

Jeremiah understood that God was the Potter and had total control over the shape of the clay. How foolish it would be for the clay to complain or rebel; "Can the pot say of the potter, 'He knows nothing'?" (Isaiah 29:16). The Potter will continue to mold the clay. If the clay begins to harden in its unfinished state, the Potter loves the clay enough to crush it down, sprinkle it with water and begin anew.

The only way for us to become all that God desires is to yield and remain moldable. We have no ability to shape ourself! The Potter is creating something eternally beautiful - we are being "conformed to the likeness of His Son" (Romans 8:29). Oh, if we could only trust that His shaping is so much better than anything we could ever create. How prideful to think we can do better!

There may be times when we have rough edges which must be removed. There may also be times when we need to be crushed down so the shaping process can start over. But we must trust the Potter and believe the results will be worth any pain or discomfort; "I consider that our present sufferings are not worth comparing with the glory that will be revealed in us" (Romans 8:18).

Our Heavenly Father is in complete (and loving) control. Let's daily be filled with His Spirit and commit our lives to His shaping process - a process which undoubtedly will last a lifetime! Let's remain moldable clay and yield to the shaping of the Potter's Hand.

WHAT WE'VE SEEN AND HEARD

How will we respond to those who doubt? What should we say to those with uncertainties, or to those who ask, "Is Jesus really the answer?"

We could begin with how the Bible is the true Word of God: "A collection of 66 books written by many different authors, during a 1500 year time period, and all with the same message." Or, we could discuss the Old Testament prophesies which were fulfilled with Jesus. We could show where Micah said the Savior would be born in Bethlehem (Micah 5:2) and where Isaiah stated He would be born of a virgin (Isaiah 7:14).

We could point to Zechariah who prophesied that our King would enter Jerusalem "gentle and riding on a donkey" (Zechariah 9:9), how David said He would be crucified; "they have pierced My hands and My feet" (Psalm 22:16), and how Isaiah said He would die for our sin; "He bore the sin of many, and made intercession for the transgressors" (Isaiah 53:12).

These are all good truths to share at the appropriate time; but when someone is doubting or searching, it's usually best to follow the example of Jesus. John the Baptist had sent messengers to ask Jesus, "Are you the one who was to come, or should we expect someone else?" (Luke 7:19).

Luke 7:21-22

"At that very time Jesus cured many who had diseases, sicknesses and evil spirits, and gave sight to many who were blind. So He replied to the messengers, 'Go back and report to John what you have seen and heard.'"

While it's good to be able to defend our faith, we will never convince anyone to believe by presenting Biblical "facts." The most convincing argument as to the truth of God's Word is to share how we've seen His Word come alive in our own life; how we've seen Jesus calm the seas and rebuke the storms, heal broken lives and answer prayers. We ought to share how we've heard Him call us to test the waters of faith and seen the waters become solid as we stepped; how we've experienced "the peace of God, which transcends all understanding" (Philippians 4:7). When God's truths become real in our daily life, they cannot be argued against!

If His truths have not yet become absolute and unquestionably real, then I urge you to press VERY close into His presence and allow His light to shine in and through you each and every day. There can be no better preparation for sharing the truth than to live the truth. Let's "prepare" to share the gospel; and when the opportunity arises, let's simply report what we've seen and heard.

TRUSTING IN HIS GRACE

In the message "What We've Seen and Heard" we were encouraged to press in close to the presence of God and share how His truths have been made real in our life. As we continue to walk with our Heavenly Father and better understand His love, we ought to experience a sense of awe which we can't help but share with others.

The complete story of Jesus Christ - which began before the creation of the world and continues for all eternity - is a love story whose central theme is grace; "For it is by grace you have been saved, through faith - and this not from yourselves, it is the gift of God" (Ephesians 2:8). The moment we believe in Jesus for the forgiveness of our sin, God looks upon us with love and welcomes us into His Family - this is His gift of Salvation! This means our Salvation is never something we earn or deserve - it is a gift of grace.

Romans 11:6

"And if by grace, then it is no longer by works; if it were, grace would no longer be grace."

If we come before our Heavenly Father thinking we can do ANYTHING which makes us deserving of Salvation, then we do not yet understand - we are not yet prepared to receive His gift. God's grace is either complete or it is no longer grace. His grace is extended to all who believe, but true belief means believing His grace is absolutely necessary AND completely sufficient.

If we truly believe, our life will produce fruit and we will do good works; "Faith, if not accompanied by action, is dead" (James 2:17). But our good works will never save us - Salvation is a gift. If we truly believe, we will desire to obediently follow; "We know that we have come to know Him if we obey His commands" (1 John 2:3). But our obedience will never save us - Salvation is a gift.

If we've never settled the issue of Salvation, then today is the day to "trust in the Lord with all your heart and lean not on your own understanding" (Proverbs 3:5). We must come before God with empty hands, acknowledge our sin and need for a Savior, and receive the gift of grace offered through Jesus.

As we then continue our walk with Christ, we learn to love Him with all our heart and strive to present our very best, bringing Him glory and honor in ALL we do. But while we walk, love, and strive, we must remember that our "best" is not what earns His favor. Our "successes" will not make us more worthy, and our "failures" will not cause us to lose His love. His gift is everything! Let's give Him everything in return as we continue to live each moment of this wondrous journey by trusting in His grace.

GUARD AGAINST THE YEAST

When God led the people of Israel out of slavery in Egypt, He told them to prepare for a quick departure by making bread without yeast. He gave instructions to remember their departure through the celebration of Passover - also called the Feast of Unleavened Bread. During this celebration there was a seven day period when yeast was not even allowed in the home: "For seven days no yeast is to be found in your houses. And whoever eats anything with yeast in it must be cut off from the community of Israel" (Exodus 12:19).

When God established the various offerings through Moses, yeast became associated with an unworthy sacrifice; "Every grain offering you bring to the Lord must be made without yeast" (Leviticus 2:11).

About 1500 years later, Jesus used the symbolism of yeast to give His disciples an important warning.

Luke 12:1

"Be on your guard against the yeast of the Pharisees, which is hypocrisy."

With this choice of words, Jesus warned that hypocrisy has the ability to contaminate our lives - and therefore the offering we present to God. The Pharisees had an outward appearance of godliness, but their hearts had compromised true worship and become contaminated; "On the outside you appear to people as righteous but on the inside you are full of hypocrisy and wickedness" (Matthew 23:28). Does our heart match what we wear on the outside?

The symbolism of yeast gives another clear warning; "A little yeast works through the whole batch of dough" (Galatians 5:9). Every day we are tempted to make compromises with the world - compromises which cause us to behave contrary to our professed beliefs. This is hypocrisy and must be avoided at all cost! Each incident seems so small - like only "a little yeast" - but soon the compromises work through all areas of our life.

The only worthy endeavor during our allotted time on earth is to present ourselves, with complete abandonment, as a living sacrifice to God; "this is your Spiritual (or reasonable) act of worship" (Romans 12:1). Our Heavenly Father is worthy of our very best - a pure and holy offering.

Let's celebrate our release from the slavery of sin by cleaning our home and removing all Spiritual compromise. Let's give our whole heart to God in loving worship and guard against ANYTHING which pulls us away. Let's fight the hypocrisy in our lives and diligently guard against the yeast.

SPOTS OF A LEOPARD

In the message "Guard Against The Yeast" we saw how Jesus warned about allowing even a little hypocrisy to enter our life. When we compromise any area of our beliefs, we are in grave danger of allowing the compromise to spread "through the whole batch of dough" (Galatians 5:9).

In the days of Jeremiah, God warned the people of Jerusalem about the destruction which was coming unless they turned from their evil ways. But the people continued in their sin and refused to listen. God gave them many opportunities to repent, but they had become comfortable in their sin and were unwilling - possibly even unable - to change.

Jeremiah 13:22-23

> *"And if you ask yourself, 'Why has this happened to me?' - it is because of your many sins. Can the Ethiopian change his skin or the leopard its spots? Neither can you do good who are accustomed to doing evil."*

One of the devastating results of sin is that it causes separation from God; and separation causes the defense against temptation to weaken. Unfortunately, a weakened defense makes it easier to continue in sin...causing further separation. The cycle of sin and separation had continued in Jerusalem until sin was viewed as normal behavior. The "yeast" had been mixed into every part of the dough and their conscience had become "seared as with a hot iron" (1 Timothy 4:2).

We need to understand this when ministering to those who are lost. People without Jesus have a difficult time recognizing their sin and certainly see no need to "change." Rather than simply pointing out their sin, which they consider "normal," we must share the love of Christ - His purpose and plan - and help lead them to faith in the Savior. Only Jesus can create true change; only His grace can reveal and remove sin.

But we must also understand this dangerous condition in our own life. Is there sin which we are beginning to view as "normal" behavior and allowing to hinder the joy of being in His presence? Is our sin forming "spots" which we now call ordinary and acceptable? Sin causes separation which leads to more sin. This cycle must be recognized and stopped!

Although we may have wandered, all hunger for change is the conviction of the Holy Spirit who is calling us to repentance - calling us to respond today and to keep our conscience from becoming seared. Let's break the cycle of sin and return to a life which glorifies our Heavenly Father in ALL we do. Let's never become so accustomed to sin that we develop the unchangeable spots of a leopard.

THIS LAST DAY

On the evening before He was crucified, Jesus ate one last meal with His disciples. For three years, the disciples had been instructed by Jesus and witnessed His miracles. He had taught them many lessons about the Kingdom of God - and about His upcoming death: "He will be handed over to the Gentiles. They will mock Him, insult Him, spit on Him, flog Him and kill Him" (Luke 18:32).

Now with less than one day to live, Jesus told His closest companions that one of them would soon betray Him; "The hand of him who is going to betray Me is with Mine on the table" (Luke 22:21). Naturally, the disciples were shocked - but their focus soon turned to trivial matters.

Luke 22:23-24

"They began to question among themselves which of them it might be who would do this. Also a dispute arose among them as to which of them was considered to be greatest."

These men were eating supper with the Creator of the Universe and witnessing the most awesome events in the history of the world. And yet, in this last day, with only a few remaining hours, their concerns drifted to matters of position and status.

It's tempting to criticize these first disciples: "How could they be so self-consumed?" But then, how often do we make this exact same mistake? With our eternal Home just around the corner, and a Savior who is willing to walk every day by our side, how often do we become absorbed in the non-eternal?

Sure, we have real responsibilities and concerns in our day-to-day walk. Our finances or health may look uncertain, the harsh words of others may offend and cause great pain; but when properly viewed against the backdrop of eternity, each worldly issue must shrink down to the trivial. If we really understood the glory we will one day see and how soon all else will fade away, we would be much less concerned about our "greatness" in the eyes of the world.

With wonderful hindsight we can say the disciples should have known their time with Jesus was short. They should have seen the events unfolding, taken advantage of every precious moment, and worshipped Him with every breath, every heartbeat, every thought, and every word - but they didn't.

And now, with the foresight given through God's Word and the guidance of His Spirit, we face the same challenge! Our Father has called us into a deep and personal relationship with Himself though faith in His Son - and our time is very, very short (much shorter than we realize). What concerns or passions will consume our time and energy? With all we have been given, what will we now do with this last day?

THE MOUNTAIN OF FAITH

When Abraham was over eighty years old, God made him a wonderful promise: "A son coming from your own body will be your heir. Look up at the heavens and count the stars - so shall your offspring be" (Genesis 15:4-5).

Many years went by without any indication that God would fulfill this promise. Finally, when Abraham was one hundred years old (and Sarah, his wife, ninety) God fulfilled His promise through the birth of Isaac. But when Isaac was a young boy, God told Abraham to sacrifice his beloved son.

Genesis 22:2

> *"Take your son, your only son, Isaac, whom you love, and go to the region of Moriah. Sacrifice him there as a burnt offering on one of the mountains I will tell you about."*

We can't even imagine receiving this type of command from God. Abraham loved Isaac; and Isaac also represented the fulfillment of God's promise. But Abraham didn't even question the apparent conflict between God's promise and His command - he simply believed and obeyed. He took Isaac and climbed the mountain, placed him on top of a pile of wood, and "took the knife to slay his son" (Genesis 22:10).

Many people speculate about the turmoil in Abraham's mind during this time, but Scripture gives no indication that Abraham ever seemed anxious or concerned. He believed in God, believed His promises, and his faith never seemed to waiver. As Abraham was about to kill his son, God stopped him and provided a ram as a substitute sacrifice (Genesis 22:13).

God put Abraham through an unimaginable test of faith - but why? The test wasn't for God - He already knew Abraham's faith! The test may have been to strengthen Abraham's faith. God often tests us as a way of refining and drawing us closer to Himself.

But I think the main reason for Abraham being asked to climb the mountain was so we would have a clear picture of what it means to believe. Belief is central to the gospel message, and the picture of Abraham allows us to truly understand what Jesus meant when He said; "whoever believes in Him shall not perish but have eternal life" (John 3:16).

God is calling us to believe - calling us to a life of faith where we have such a strong assurance of His presence that He is all we need...all we value and hold dear. Let's give ourselves completely to Him, without ANY reservation - let's truly believe! Let's give Him ALL our heart and be willing to sacrifice ALL for His glory and honor. Let's once and for all climb the mountain of faith.

LISTEN AS WE CLIMB

In the message "The Mountain of Faith" we were encouraged to believe with a faith secure enough to surrender ALL to our Lord and Savior. We saw an example of this faith in Abraham as he was given a son and then told to surrender him as a burnt offering; "Take your son, your only son, Isaac, whom you love, and go to the region of Moriah. Sacrifice him there as a burnt offering on one of the mountains I will tell you about" (Genesis 22:2).

Without any debate or even apparent doubt, Abraham set out with Isaac and a bundle of wood and began to obediently climb the mountain of faith. What special quality did Abraham have which allowed him to make such a climb? Only one! He believed God; "Abram believed the Lord, and He credited it to him as righteousness" (Genesis 15:6). Clearly, belief is tied directly to trust and obedience. Abraham believed God had a purpose for giving him such a command and he immediately obeyed.

Many of us are longing for clear direction from God. Although we probably pray that His direction doesn't require the sacrifice of Abraham, we're ready to follow and are in a mode of waiting. Waiting can be very frustrating and sometimes cause us to speed up God's timing. But we must continue to patiently seek

17

the Lord, trust there is a purpose in the wait, continue to grow and mature, and be obedient to the things God has already given us to do. His direction will come - and when it does, we must be prepared to follow.

There is a mature part of Abraham's climb we often overlook. Perhaps if Isaac had been born ten years earlier, Abraham would not have been mature enough to make such a climb. You see, Abraham had learned to ALWAYS keep his eyes on the Lord - always listen for His leading - even once his direction appeared clear.

Genesis 22: 9-11

"He bound his son Isaac and laid him on the altar, on top of the wood. Then he reached out his hand and took the knife to slay his son. But the angel of the Lord called out to him from heaven, 'Abraham! Abraham!' 'Here I am,' he replied."

What would have happened if Abraham had become so focused on "the mission" that he failed to listen for the voice of the Lord? Abraham was being obedient to the call of God; but right at the point of absolute obedience, God changed direction; "Do not lay a hand on the boy" (Genesis 22:12).

The call of God is not a one time event - it's an ongoing, moment by moment relationship of love. We are never sent on a mission away from the presence of the Lord. We are called to follow, making the journey hand in hand, and step by step. Let's continue to grow ever closer to our Heavenly Father. Let's trust Him more, love Him more, and always, always, always, listen as we climb.

FAITH TO MOVE MOUNTAINS

In the message "The Mountain of Faith" we saw the faith of Abraham as God told him to climb the mountain and sacrifice Isaac. But, more importantly, we saw this as a picture of what it means to truly believe. Jesus said, "whoever believes in Him shall not perish but have eternal life" (John 3:16), but true belief clearly implies a willingness to obediently follow.

The gift of eternal life is given to those who have faith in Jesus for the forgiveness of sin. This precious gift is never linked to a specific amount of faith; rather, the only requirement of the gospel is that our faith be genuine. In fact, Jesus stated that a small amount of faith can accomplish more than we can imagine.

Matthew 17:20

"If you have faith as small as a mustard seed, you can say to this mountain, 'Move from here to there' and it will move. Nothing will be impossible for you."

This is amazing! Jesus used the example of a mustard seed because it was the smallest seed known. A few chapters later, He made a similar statement; "If you have faith and do not doubt...you can say to this mountain, 'Go throw yourself into the sea,' and it will be done" (Matthew 21:21). If we are a child of God then we have already been given sufficient faith by Jesus, "the author and perfecter of our faith" (Hebrews 12:2). There is therefore NO obstacle which cannot be cast aside!

Of course, genuine faith also implies an alignment with the will of God. Jesus even said "He can do only what He sees His Father doing" (John 5:19). This is why we don't see physical mountains moving around today - it's not in the will of God. However, it's most definitely in God's will that we move all mountains which threaten to block our path toward Him or hinder His plan for our life.

If we really believe, we ought to be living our life according to His truth and the faith we have been given! Though we may face mountains in our job, relationships, finances, health, kids, or parents; though we may face temptations or addictions which appear impossible to conquer; though we may battle a low self esteem which says we can't, we must believe the Word of God is true! "With God ALL things are possible" (Matthew 19:26). Though we may not understand, we must believe, in faith, that God is infinitely greater than the bounds of our understanding. We are not walking alone and NO problem is beyond His ability to direct.

If we desire to live the full life God intends - the life that honors Him with every move and even every breath - then God's Word must become our foundation. Whatever problems we face, we must fall on our knees with humble submission to His will and seek His face in prayer. Then we must rise up and step forward without doubt, and, in His strength, believe we have been given the faith to move mountains.

IN SPITE OF OUR CHAINS

In the message "Faith to Move Mountains" we saw that, though our faith may appear small, all genuine believers in Jesus Christ have the faith to move any and all mountains which stand between us and a close relationship with our Heavenly Father. HOWEVER...Not all trials represent mountains which must be moved! Many things we view as obstacles are perfectly aligned with God's plan.

Our Christian walk never promises freedom from trouble. In fact, Jesus promised us just the opposite; "In this world you will have trouble" (John 16:33a). Fortunately, Jesus immediately followed these words with a message of hope; "But take heart! I have overcome the world" (John 16:33b). Though trials may come and remain much longer than we'd like, we can still be set free by abiding in The One who has overcome.

The Apostle Paul had many trials during his ministry: "Five times I received from the Jews the forty lashes minus one. Three times I was beaten with rods, once I was stoned, three times I was shipwrecked, I spent a night and a day in the open sea" (2 Corinthians 11:24-25). But Paul was able to keep his trials in proper perspective by focusing on what was eternally relevant; "I consider that our present sufferings are not worth comparing with the glory that will be revealed in us" (Romans 8:18).

Toward the end of his ministry, Paul was arrested for the "offense" of preaching the gospel. While awaiting trial in Rome, Paul spent two years under the guard of a Roman soldier and wrote a wonderful letter of encouragement to the Philippians "Rejoice in the Lord always. I will say it again: Rejoice!" (Philippians 4:4). Though he was confined, Paul allowed himself to be used by God to encourage many others toward an increase in their faith.

Philippians 1:14

"Because of my chains, most of the brothers in the Lord have been encouraged to speak the word of God more courageously and fearlessly."

Every time we experience a trial, the world watches to see the substance of our faith. Often, there is no better way to minister to others than to simply praise God in the middle of our own trials. The best way to show that God is real is by making Him real in our own life.

Let's take a new look at our trials. Some are truly mountains which must be moved; but others are simply the chains we must joyfully endure for the sake of the gospel. Let's turn what the enemy meant for harm into something which glorifies God. Let's encourage others to draw nearer to a loving Father as we praise Him with all our heart...in spite of our chains.

STRAIN TOWARD THE VINE

Our life in these mortal bodies will always fall short of God's standard. From the moment sin entered the world, we've been unable to satisfy God's requirement of perfection. But, knowing our weakness, God gave His Son as a sacrifice to perfect those who believe; "By one sacrifice He has made perfect forever those who are being made holy" (Hebrews 10:14). Faith in the sacrifice of Jesus makes us perfect forever - this is the gracious gift of Salvation; "it is by grace you have been saved, through faith" (Ephesians 2:8).

The grace of God makes us perfect the moment we are saved; but, for the rest of our days on this earth, we are in the process of "being made holy." This is why Paul, who freely writes about the gift of grace, can also exhort us to a life free of sin; "Do not let sin reign in your mortal body so that you obey its evil desires" (Romans 6:12). Paul understood that, though we have become "perfect forever," we have also been called to a high standard of holiness. He therefore refers to his life after Salvation as a race to be won; "Forgetting what is behind and straining toward what is ahead, I press on toward the goal to win the prize for which God has called me" (Philippians 3:12-14).

The picture of a well-conditioned athlete straining toward the finish line can be a wonderful motivator. However, when we press and strain toward the wrong goal - or with our own strength - we will soon become fatigued and discouraged. We are in a race, but we must allow Jesus to establish the goal as well as the route to be run. The goal of a Christian life must always be to produce fruit that glorifies God; "This is to My Father's glory, that you bear much fruit" (John 15:8). And the route of fruit production must ALWAYS be through the vine of Christ.

John 15:4-5

"No branch can bear fruit by itself; it must remain in the vine. Neither can you bear fruit unless you remain in Me. I am the vine; you are the branches. If a man remains in Me and I in him, he will bear much fruit; apart from Me you can do nothing."

We are called to produce fruit by living a life of holiness and bringing glory and honor to God in all we do. However, fruit can only grow if we remain intimately attached to the vine - a branch cannot produce anything by itself! In our own strength we cannot produce holiness or ANYTHING esteemed by God. But when we allow the life of the vine to flow through our veins, we WILL produce a bounty of fruit.

Let's attach firmly to the vine of Jesus Christ and allow Him to flow though every area of our life. Let's live each day in the holy presence of God and produce baskets of fruit for His glory and honor. Let's run to win the race as we press and strain toward the vine.

SECURE IN HIS PRESENCE

Jehoiakim was king of Judah just prior to the first Babylonian invasion in 605 B.C.. He had become comfortable in the security of the palace, and an alliance with the Egyptians made him feel even more protected. But Jehoiakim led the people of Judah further away from God; "he did evil in the eyes of the Lord, just as his fathers had done" (2 Kings 23:37).

God sent the prophet Jeremiah to warn Jehoiakim and the people of Judah that disaster would come if they did not repent; "If you do not listen to Me and follow My law..., then I will make this city an object of cursing among all the nations of the earth" (Jeremiah 26:4,6). But with his every need and desire fulfilled - and with all his fears removed - Jehoiakim did not see a reason to listen to God.

Jeremiah 22:21

> *"I warned you when you felt secure, but you said, 'I will not listen!' This has been your way from your youth; you have not obeyed."*

We spend the majority of our lives building security in our job, finances, and relationships. But security within the world system is extremely shallow and deceptive; "Do not store up for yourselves treasures {security} on earth, where moth and rust destroy, where thieves break in and steal" (Matthew 6:19). We ought to be thankful for every one of our earthly blessings, but we should NEVER receive our "security" from the world. Our complete dependence must always remain on our Heavenly Father, and our eyes and ears continually open to His leading.

Our daily walk is made one slow step at a time as we "trust in the Lord with all your heart and lean not on your own understanding" (Proverbs 3:5). Usually, we are allowed to see only the next few steps; "Your Word is a lamp unto my feet, and a light for my path" (Psalm 119:105). But our true security, peace and comfort, comes from simply knowing we're on His path, not from feeling we control the direction or pace of the journey.

This security begins with faith in Jesus Christ and builds on a pure love which flows from the innermost part of our heart. Even activities such as church attendance, Bible study, or work in various ministries mean nothing without a faith based love; and these well-intended actions become a false security when they replace the need to abide in the presence of God or daily seek His direction.

Let's not allow our lives to develop a sense of security which shuts out the need for God and the absolute hunger for His presence. Our walk of faith will always require stepping into the unknown where all we have is what He provides - and a loving trust is confident that His provision is enough! Let's lean on Him, love Him, and draw ever closer. Let's seek true security by only being secure in His presence.

MISPLACED TRUST

In the message "Secure In His Presence" we were encouraged to guard against anything which takes away from our complete dependence on our Heavenly Father. We saw how worldly security can sometimes cause us to close our eyes and ears to God's leading. Becoming secure in the world is to also place our trust in the things of the world. David made this mistake and it cost him dearly.

God described David as "a man after My own heart" (Acts 13:22). David clearly saw God working in his life. When he went to fight Goliath with only stones and a sling, he knew to trust in the strength offered by God; "All those gathered here will know that it is not by sword or spear that the Lord saves; for the battle is the Lord's" (1 Samuel 17:47). God continued to protect David through his trials with Saul and later led him through many military victories as the king of Israel. But toward the end of his reign, David began to trust the world's definition of power and might.

1 Chronicles 21:1-2

"Satan rose up against Israel and incited David to take a census of Israel. So David said to Joab and the commanders of the troops, 'Go and count the Israelites. Then

report back to me so that I may know how many there are.'"

God allowed Satan to tempt David because there was still deep rooted pride in David that needed to be revealed. There was nothing inherently wrong with counting the people - after all, when God led the nation of Israel out of Egypt, He told Moses; "Take a census of the whole Israelite community" (Numbers 1:2). But David had become very "self" reliant and had placed his trust in his own strength and abilities. He became focused on his resources - the number of men who were able to fight - rather than keeping his eyes and ears on the true Commander of ALL battles.

David recognized and confessed his sin: "I have sinned greatly by doing this. Now, I beg You, take away the guilt" (1 Chronicles 21:8). Though David's sin was forgiven, God still enforced severe consequences; "So the Lord sent a plague on Israel, and seventy thousand men of Israel fell dead" (1 Chronicles 21:14). As the leader of God's chosen people, David was expected to set a clear example of complete trust.

God wants and expects the total devotion of our heart. Devotion will always mean love and worship; but it also must include our sustained and unwavering trust. Our Heavenly Father establishes our path and provides all the necessary strength to achieve the victory He desires. He simply asks that we trust only in Him and continue to follow where He leads. Let's give Him ALL the glory and honor as we keep our eyes forever focused on Christ and guard against the sin of misplaced trust.

TOOLS OF THE TEACHER

In the days of the prophet Jeremiah, God's chosen people had turned away to worship other gods. But God longed for His children to return and worship Him as the One True God. The Israelites had been warned for many years and now God used a foreign king as His tool for discipline and instruction.

Jeremiah 27:6

> *"Now I will hand all your countries over to My servant Nebuchadnezzar king of Babylon; I will make even the wild animals subject to him."*

God reminded the people that He alone was almighty and in control of world events. But He also revealed their sinful pride as He required them to yield to His discipline in order to survive; "Bow your neck under the yoke of the king of Babylon and you will live" (Jeremiah 27:12). Many chose to die rather than to trust God and submit to His instruction.

Nebuchadnezzar did not even acknowledge God at this point in his life - and yet, God called him "My servant." It was God's plan to use this non-believing foreigner to teach His children some very important (and painful) lessons. God's Hand of discipline is firm, but His Hand is always directed with a loving purpose.

29

Pride was keeping His children away, and it needed to be removed by any tool available.

Being adopted into God's family through the gift of Salvation is a one time event. Through faith in the sacrifice of Jesus for the forgiveness of our sin, we receive His grace and become "a new creation" (2 Corinthians 5:17). However, learning to truly live for God and become "conformed to the likeness of His Son" (Romans 8:29), is an on-going process which will last all the rest of our days.

There is so much our Heavenly Father desires for us to understand - so many lessons He wants us to learn - and yet, all the lessons seem nearly identical. He desires a continual and intimate fellowship; He wants us to learn to trust Him and love Him with all our heart, soul, mind, and strength (Mark 12:30).

As we open our life to God's teaching, we must allow Him to instruct us using the tools of His choice. His lessons are often taught using the most unlikely messengers and through the worst of circumstances; but His lessons always contain a lasting sweetness.

No matter what we face today, let's look for the lesson God is teaching. Circumstances in our work, home, or even place of worship may often become hot with friction; but these sources of abrasion may very well be the tools God is using to mold us and draw us closer to His side - because He loves us and desires for us to learn to trust and love Him more. Let's praise Him for His continued loving instruction. Let's embrace the shaping process and be thankful for ALL the tools of The Teacher.

RETURN TO GIVE THANKS

One day when Jesus was traveling from Galilee to Jerusalem, ten men with leprosy approached Him and called out; "Jesus, Master, have pity on us!" (Luke 17:13). Jesus didn't immediate heal the lepers; rather, He gave them a simple instruction; "Go, show yourselves to the priests" (Luke 17:14).

A leper would only present himself to a priest if he believed the leprosy was gone. The priests had the authority to declare a diseased person ceremonially clean and able to return home (Leviticus 14). Therefore, the lepers demonstrated great faith when they followed Jesus' command; "And as they went, they were cleansed" (Luke 17:14). Notice that the lepers had to take action before they were healed, their action was a demonstration of their faith.

Though all ten lepers had been cleansed of their terrible disease, only one returned to give thanks; "He threw himself at Jesus' feet and thanked Him" (Luke 17:16). Jesus responded with a very convicting question.

Luke 17:17

"Jesus asked, 'Were not all ten cleansed? Where are the other nine?'"

I wonder if we really understand the degree to which we have been healed and made clean; "God made us alive with Christ even when we were dead in transgression" (Ephesians 2:5). We were DEAD, and He made us alive with Christ - that's serious healing!! Our Heavenly Father reached down in love and provided a way for complete restoration when we didn't even have the ability to cry out for help; "While we were still sinners, Christ died for us" (Romans 5:8) - that's serious love!!

His Hand guided us toward healing through His Son and His Hand continues to heal in countless ways on our daily walk. Every time relationships are restored, His hand has healed; when conflicts are resolved, His hand has healed; and when He lovingly welcomes us back after we have wandered from His presence, His hand has healed.

But do we return to thank Him? Or are we as the other nine lepers who go on our way and forget the One to whom we owe our very lives.

The one leper who returned threw himself at Jesus' feet. If we knew how deathly ill we are without Christ and how completely He has healed our soul, we would not only throw ourselves at His feet, but we would remain and refuse to ever leave. Let's live each day in the presence of God and continually come before Him with hearts overflowing with thanksgiving and praise. Let's remember our divine healing and ALWAYS be the one who will return to give thanks.

ARISE AND WALK

To grow as a Christian means to become closer and develop a more intimate relationship with God. This relationship begins when we are born into His family - when we ask Him to forgive our sins through faith in Jesus and begin what is intended to be an eternal communion of love. He desires for us to trust Him in ALL things and pray to Him on all occasions; "In everything, by prayer and petition, with thanksgiving, present your requests to God" (Philippians 4:6).

Jesus promised that our prayers will be heard and answered; "Ask and you will receive, and your joy will be complete" (John 16:24). But as we lift up our requests, we can sometimes become confused by God's response. We often perceive His answers to be slow in arriving, or we're disappointed with His reply; we even begin to doubt if God even hears our prayers.

But we must remember that we have entered into an eternal relationship with the Sovereign Creator of the Universe! Underlying all our prayers must be the firm belief that "in all things, God works for the good of those who love Him" (Romans 8:28). God always has a plan, and His plan is very, very good! We must trust that His answer to our prayers will meet our true need (and fulfill our deepest desire) much better than we could ever hope or imagine.

A short time after Jesus was crucified, Peter and John were confronted by a crippled man sitting beside the Temple gate begging for money.

Acts 3:6

"Then Peter said, 'Silver or gold I do not have, but what I have I give you. In the name of Jesus Christ of Nazareth, walk.'"

Until that day, the crippled man had never walked a single step. In his limited view of the world, the only hope he had for a better life was to be given a little money by those passing by. His request was limited by what he could see and understand - limited by his faith.

Our loving Father always hears our prayers - and He always answers. His answer to prayer is either yes, no, or wait...and sometimes He answers with, "Here my child, I have something much better for you."

God's view of our needs (and His view of the entire world) is much higher and grander than our own. We generally see our need as the solution to some short term problem, but our true need is always to grow by drawing closer and loving Him more. Let's take our eyes off the crutches we think will "fix" our problem and look instead to the One who is calling, "Trust Me and come into My presence as you arise and walk!"

PUT IT INTO PRACTICE

Paul's letter to the Philippians is one hundred and four verses filled with encouragement and joy. Paul didn't write this letter to explain deep theology or to deal with any particular sin. Rather, his purpose was to express love for his friends and to encourage them (and us) to live a joy-filled Christian life.

In chapter one, Paul encourages us that God's work in us WILL continue; "He who began a good work in you will carry it on to completion" (1:6). In chapter two, we are encouraged to "do everything without complaining or arguing" (2:14).

In chapter three, Paul inspires us to be forward-looking in our walk with Christ; "Forgetting what is behind and straining toward what is ahead, I press on toward the goal" (3:13-14). Finally, in chapter four, Paul writes some of my personal favorites; "Rejoice in the Lord always!" (4:4); "I have learned the secret of being content in any and every situation" (4:12); and, "I can do everything through Him who gives me strength" (4:13).

But buried within these wonderful words of encouragement is probably the most valuable and applicable message for our daily journey with Christ.

Philippians 4:9

"Whatever you have learned or received or heard from me, or seen in me - put it into practice. And the God of peace will be with you."

Paul had the gospel message living in him and shining through him every moment of every day. But he never would have learned "the secret" of rejoicing and being content in all situations if he had just learned "about" the gospel. Although it's wise, and very useful, to study and even memorize God's Word, His peace and contentment - His joy - will never be real until we actually apply His Word to our life on a daily basis: "Do not merely listen to the word, and so deceive yourselves. Do what it says" (James 1:22).

We must NEVER be just hearers of the Word who become puffed up with Bible knowledge. We must never preach Biblical truths yet fail to apply these truths in our own life and draw ever closer to our Heavenly Father. Jesus accused many of the Jews around Him of making this same mistake: "You diligently study the Scriptures because you think that by them you possess eternal life. These are the Scriptures that testify about Me, yet you refuse to come to Me to have life" (John 5:39-40).

Let's never stop with just loving His Word or His "activities." Let's love HIM with all our heart, soul, mind, and strength; and express our love through faith in Jesus Christ and obedience to the leading of His Spirit, as we take what we daily receive and put it into practice.

STAND FIRM IN THE GAP

In the final years of the southern kingdom of Israel, God warned He was going to use the king of Babylon to discipline the people unless they returned to Him with a heart of worship. The people failed to repent and the invasion of Jerusalem began.

Ezekiel was a prophet to those taken captive during the Babylonian attacks. Through Ezekiel, God explained why He was allowing Jerusalem to be destroyed. He said the people had rebelled and drifted far; but His anger seemed mostly directed at the leaders who failed to point the way: "{The priests} do not distinguish between the holy and the common; they teach that there is no difference between the unclean and the clean" (Ezekiel 22:26). In addition, God said the prophets were covering up the sins of the priests; "They whitewash their deeds for them by false visions and lying divinations" (Ezekiel 22:28).

God searched, but found no one who was willing to lead the people into a life of pure and holy worship - a life which recognized God as Lord of ALL and prayed without ceasing for His guidance and protection.

Ezekiel 22:30-31

"I looked for a man among them who

would build up the wall and stand before me in the gap on behalf of the land so I would not have to destroy it, but I found none. So I will pour out my wrath on them and consume them with my fiery anger."

As in the days of Ezekiel, Spiritual walls are crumbling all around us. We have whitewashed sin in the name of tolerance, and we have lost our passion for holiness and worship in the busyness of materialism and worldly advancement. And tragically, many of our churches are filled with compromise and fail to point the way to truth. The result is many lives filled with Spiritual gaps - areas vulnerable to grave attack by the enemy.

We must repair our own walls through repentance, forgiveness, and daily drawing nearer to the presence of God. But we must also look for "gaps" in the walls of those around us and commit to standing firm with prayer, encouragement, and time, until strength returns and walls are repaired. We must be ones who live without compromise and faithfully point the way to true worship and a life which glorifies God in all we do.

We must continue to stand in the gap for as long as it takes the relationship of a friend to be restored, the strength of a pastor to be renewed, the heart of a loved one to be transformed, or the life of a prodigal child to return home. God's words through Ezekiel are harsh; but God didn't give up on the people until the people gave up on each other. It's not too late if we continue to point the way; there is still hope if we will stand firm in the gap.

NEVER LOSE HOPE

In the message "Stand Firm in The Gap" we were encouraged to continue in prayer and minister to the needs of others; to stand in the gap for those who need protection against enemy attacks. We saw our responsibility to stand for as long as necessary. This requires perseverance and complete trust in God. It can be difficult when we continue to "stand" but God appears slow to respond. We can also become extremely discouraged when we think we understand HOW He should respond.

Lazarus had become sick to the point of death. His sisters were standing in the gap by ministering to his needs; they even sent word to Jesus in hopes that He would help.

John 11:4-6

"When He heard this, Jesus said, 'This sickness will not end in death. No, it is for God's glory so that God's Son may be glorified through it.' Jesus loved Martha and her sister and Lazarus. Yet when He heard that Lazarus was sick, He stayed where He was two more days."

Jesus did not immediately respond - and during this delay, Lazarus died. Yet this tragedy was for God's glory. When Jesus finally arrived, He raised Lazarus from the dead and taught an important message: "I am the resurrection and the life. He who believes in Me will live, even though he dies" (John 11:25).

Lazarus and his sisters would have preferred a healing during the early stage of the sickness - but that was not God's plan. His plan included much more than the temporary suffering of one family. His plan was to teach many people, through many generations, to this very day and beyond, that He was the sure way to eternal life. His plan was perfect, with perfect timing.

We are all given opportunities to serve by meeting the needs of others. But as we serve, we must NEVER take our eyes off our Heavenly Father. Our "job" is to stand in the gap before Him and minister in the manner His Spirit directs - it is never our responsibility to "fix" the people or circumstances we have been called to serve. If we will faithfully serve as He directs - working outward while looking upward - we will find that God uses our ministry effort to work on many issues in our own life. Most of the issues are ones we never even knew we had; "Trust in Him at all times, O people; pour out your hearts to Him, for God is our refuge" (Psalm 62:8)

When our area of service seems out of control - when the need seems to outpace our ability to serve and God seems slow to respond - we must continue to trust Him with all our heart. These times of testing will draw us closer to God as we abandon ALL into His sovereign care. He alone knows His plan - and His plan remains perfect. Let's continue to trust Him and serve as He directs. Let's continue with our eyes fixed on God, and never lose hope!

THESE ARE GOD'S BATTLES

During the time of King Jehoshaphat (approximately 860 BC), several armies began to invade the land of Judah. Being greatly outnumbered, Jehoshaphat called for a nation-wide time of fasting and prayer to seek guidance from God: "O our God, will You not judge them? For we have no power to face this vast army that is attacking us. We do not know what to do, but our eyes are upon You" (2 Chronicles 20:12).

The king needed to formulate a plan. He was the appointed leader and responsible for the safety of his people. King Jehoshaphat's "plan" was to place the fate of the entire nation into the hands of God. Many see such action as weakness, but it took great strength to recognize he was powerless - even greater strength to know where to turn and Who to trust!

God answered King Jehoshaphat's cry for help through a Levite named Jahaziel.

2 Chronicles 20:14-15

"Then the Spirit of the Lord came upon Jahaziel...'Listen, King Jehoshaphat and all who live in Judah and Jerusalem! This is what the Lord says to you: "Do not be afraid or discouraged because of this

vast army. For the battle is not yours, but God's."'"

This is great comfort when we face trials which appear much bigger than anything we can handle: we can rest in the fact that our battles belong to God. But there is more to the story! God didn't tell Jehoshaphat to just sit in his tent while the battle was won, He gave specific instructions to confidently stand before the enemy.

2 Chronicles 20:16-17

"Tomorrow march down against them...{But} you will not have to fight this battle. Take up your positions; stand firm and see the deliverance the Lord will give you, O Judah and Jerusalem. Do not be afraid; do not be discouraged. Go out to face them tomorrow, and the Lord will be with you.'"

It's inevitable that our life will contain such battles - many are facing overwhelming battles right now. As with everything we encounter on our Christian walk, battles have a purpose. Many times the purpose of our battle is to understand a fundamental truth: "Apart from Me you can do nothing" (John 15:5). Reaching the end of our own strength is our real battle - turning to God and trusting Him for every step of our walk is the real victory!

As we trust Him with all our heart and seek counsel in His presence, He will tell us where to march and where to stand. Let's boldly follow our Lord each and every day and refuse to become discouraged. He is in absolute control...for these are God's battles!

SERVE WITH HUMILITY

John the Baptist was born with a single purpose: "to make ready a people prepared to receive the Lord" (Luke 1:17). He was chosen for service before he was conceived and was "filled with the Holy Spirit even from birth" (Luke 1:15). John was so obedient to his calling that Jesus said, "Among those born of women, there is no one greater than John" (Luke 7:28). But John also knew his position within God's Kingdom - he had come to serve.

John 1:26-27

> "'I baptize with water,' John replied, 'but among you stands one you do not know. He is the one who comes after me, the thongs of whose sandals I am not worthy to untie.'"

John had been given his assignment and was empowered by the Holy Spirit to accomplish his tasks: he was a servant preparing the way for the King. John was the greatest man ever born of a woman; and yet, in his humility, he felt unworthy to even untie the sandals of Christ.

True humility is not simply defined by a low self-image, it is the natural condition of our spirit when we begin to understand who we really are...and Who God really is! John felt unworthy because he had been given a glimpse of the unfathomable greatness and holiness of his Lord. As he stood in the presence of Perfection, there was only one response; "He must become greater, I must become less" (John 3:30).

When we know that Jesus is on the throne, "at God's right hand" (1 Peter 3:22), and that He will reign for all eternity, we begin to see our life in the proper perspective. He is infinitely perfect and worthy of infinite love, worship, and service. We live and breathe purely by His grace; we are but "a mist that appears for a little while and then vanishes" (James 4:14).

And yet, we are a mist with a purpose. We have been empowered by the Holy Spirit with the necessary tools to victoriously serve. Though our offering will always be imperfect, and far less than He deserves, it will be pleasing and acceptable if we give Him our ALL, give Him our best, and give from the innermost part of our heart.

Let's continue to love Him with all our heart, give Him our absolute very best, and walk down the path He lays before us. Let's serve obediently, boldly, and victoriously...but let's also lift the Name of Jesus higher and higher and serve with humility.

INTENDED FOR GOOD

Joseph's life was filled with one difficult situation after another. By the time he was a teenager, his brothers had developed an intense hatred toward him. Their hatred led to an attempt to take his life - but rather than kill him, they sold young Joseph into slavery (Genesis 37). And then, as a slave, Joseph was falsely accused of rape and thrown into jail (Genesis 39).

It's never really explained how Joseph learned to trust God - but he did! He could have become very discouraged when he became a slave, but somehow Joseph adjusted to his circumstances and thrived; "The Lord was with Joseph and he prospered" (Genesis 39:2). When tempted with sexual sin by Potiphar's wife, he kept himself pure because he did not want to "sin against God" (Genesis 39:9). But false accusations still sent him into prison.

Even after spending several years in jail, Joseph continued to place his complete trust in God. When asked to interpret Pharaoh's dreams, Joseph risked his freedom and rightly gave all the glory and praise to God rather than take credit for himself; "I cannot do it, but God will give Pharaoh the answer he desires" (Genesis 41:16).

Joseph was rewarded with much more than his freedom; he was placed in charge of the entire land of Egypt during a great famine. He was also reunited with his family and able to keep them from certain starvation. Several years later, after their father died, Joseph's brothers came and fearfully asked for his forgiveness. Joseph could have taken great revenge, but he continued to demonstrate his understanding of how God cares for His children.

Genesis 50:19-20

"Joseph said to them, 'Don't be afraid. Am I in the place of God? You intended to harm me, but God intended it for good to accomplish what is now being done, the saving of many lives.'"

When Joseph was sold into slavery, he had no idea of God's awesome plan. He would spend many years in jail before receiving even a hint of God's purpose. But God is ALWAYS at work in the lives of those who love Him. Joseph's life must encourage us to draw near to God during times of hardship - to continue trusting and honoring Him in all we do...no matter what our circumstances!

We all go through "dungeon" seasons when life seems to take unplanned and seemingly "unfair" turns. We all, at times, feel abandoned and alone: "Has God forgotten me? Does He no longer care?" We may not understand why things happen the way they do, but if we will continue to love Him with all our heart and consistently trust Him in and through all our trials, we can be certain (and we will one day see) that God is in control and our situation is truly intended for good.

NEVER FORGET

It had been forty years since Moses led the Israelites out of Egypt. During their years of wandering in the desert, God demonstrated His faithfulness as well as His holiness. Now, as the people were finally ready to cross the Jordan river into the promised land of Canaan, Moses gave one last encouragement.

Deuteronomy 6:10-12

"When the Lord your God brings you into the land He swore to your fathers - a land with large, flourishing cities you did not build, houses filled with all kinds of good things you did not provide, wells you did not dig, and vineyards and olive groves you did not plant - then when you eat and are satisfied, be careful that you do not forget the Lord, who brought you out of Egypt, out of the land of slavery."

We have all lived in the land of slavery - a land where we were controlled by sin. We were born as slaves, but Jesus came to set us free: "Though you used to be slaves to sin, you wholeheartedly obeyed the form of teaching to which you were entrusted. You have been set free" (Romans 6:17-18).

While we were still lost in our sinful condition, Jesus gave His life as a sacrifice (payment) for our sin - but He also broke the chains which kept us slaves to sin. Though we still struggle, we need not be mastered if we have placed our faith in Jesus and daily submit to the leading of His Spirit. His sacrifice provides a way to be "heirs of God and co-heirs with Christ" (Romans 8:17). This IS a victorious life!

Yes we have been set free! But we did nothing to earn this freedom. We did not dig a well of righteousness or plant a field of forgiveness. Our "promised land" of freedom is a gift, given by a loving Father to those who believe.

As we continue on our Christian walk, with its many peaks and valleys, twists and turns, we often forget. We become discouraged over trivial matters which are quickly fading away and forget the gift of eternal life we have been given. We wander in the dry desert of ungrateful hearts and ask, "Where is God?" We forget the joy we once had of abiding in His presence and forget His promise to always be near; "Never will I leave you; never will I forsake you" (Hebrews 13:5).

Through God's precious gift, we have an eternity to worship our Heavenly Father. This alone should give us reason to praise His Name with every breath and live a life holy and pleasing to Him. Whether we are currently in a time of crushing trials or unparalleled peace, we must continually remember from where we were rescued. His gift is a blessing we can hardly comprehend! And as we draw near and give Him all of our heart, His grace continues to bless us even more. Let's worship with a thankful heart, glorify His Name in ALL we do, and be careful to never forget.

PRECIOUS IN HIS SIGHT

In the message "Never Forget" we saw that God's gift of Salvation through faith in Jesus is our greatest blessing - a blessing we must never forget as we tend to become discouraged. In the beginning, "God created man in His own image" (Genesis 1:27). Then, when sin entered the world and man became separated from God, "He gave His one and only Son, that whoever believes in Him shall not perish but have eternal life" (John 3:16).

This is the greatest love story in all history; "While we were still {lost} sinners, Christ died for us" (Romans 5:8). He died for you and me, and also for all those other lost sinners scattered around us. Jesus Christ, "who being in very nature God" (Philippians 2:6), was born in a dirty stable; "He made Himself nothing, taking the very nature of a servant" (Philippians 2:7). He lived His life with the single purpose of dying so that ALL who believe could be eternally restored to the Father; "the result of one act of righteousness was justification that brings life for all men" (Romans 5:18).

God loves us VERY much! And He doesn't just love those who love Him in return or faithfully serve Him - He loves ALL. Yes, He hates sin and will one day judge with an eternal damnation all who fail to believe; but His love - His offer of Salvation - extends to all...even to our noisy neighbor and difficult co-worker, to our obnoxious family members and the disrespectful kids who wear "strange" clothes.

God's love is so much a part of who He is, and of who we ought to be, that Jesus commands us by His example: "Love one another. As I have loved you, so you must love one another" (John 13:34). We are to love as Jesus loved; and as if this was too difficult a concept for our finite minds, we are commanded to love in terms we can all understand.

Galatians 5:14

"The entire law is summed up in a single command: 'Love your neighbor as yourself.'"

God wants us to love others primarily because He loves them and desires His love to be expressed through us! He encouraged this love by creating us with a natural capacity for love. When we are hungry we feed ourself; when we are hurt we care for ourself; and when we are down, we pray to be lifted up. These are natural expressions of love - the same love God desires us to show to ALL.

Let's evaluate our thoughts, words, and actions in terms of their effect on others. Are we encouraging or adding burdens? Are we building up or tearing down? Are we bringing others closer to Jesus or pushing them further away? Are we as loving to others as we are to ourself? Let's be His hands, feet, and voice of love in the world around us. Let's begin to see others as through His eyes; and remember, we are ALL precious in His sight.

ACCORDING TO YOUR WILL

On the night before He was crucified, Jesus went to the Garden of Gethsemane to pray. The thought of what would take place in the next 24 hours caused Jesus to be deeply troubled; "My soul is overwhelmed with sorrow to the point of death" (Mark 14:34).

Being fully God, Jesus knew exactly what was about to take place and exactly why it had to occur. But being fully Man, the foreknowledge of the rejection, physical pain, and spiritual separation from the Father was nearly unbearable.

Mark 14:36

"'Abba, Father,' He said, 'everything is possible for You. Take this cup from Me. Yet not what I will, but what You will.'"

Jesus cried out and asked for the plan to be changed; and yet, His greater desire was for the Father's will to be done. Earlier in His ministry, Jesus taught us this same principle; "This, then, is how you should pray: 'Our Father in Heaven, hallowed be Your name, Your Kingdom come, Your will be done on earth as it is in Heaven'" (Matthew 6:9-10). Even with an absolute understanding of what He must endure, Jesus' sole desire was to glorify the Father by walking the path placed before Him;

51

"I have brought You glory on earth by completing the work You gave Me to do" (John 17:4).

This is the example we ought to follow all through our life; we should present ourself to the Father, fully prepared to serve, and be completely emptied of our own desires. When we have allowed Him to be the only possessor of our heart, He will fill us with His Spirit and accomplish His perfect will through our life. When our life is ordered and directed only by His will, we will receive blessings from above which bring far greater joy than the fulfillment of ANY flesh-directed desire.

This is one of the mysterious "secrets" of the Christian walk. We were created to be in fellowship with God - to glorify Him and enjoy His presence for all eternity. We may spend a lifetime chasing what we believe will bring us a sense of fulfillment, but we will never be truly content until we rest in His arms and submit to His ways.

What cup have we been given to drink; what seemingly unbearable burden have we been given to carry? Have we been asking, even demanding, that the burdens be taken from us, or are we yielding to the Father's will and being determined to glorify Him in all we do? Let's come to His table ready and willing to serve; but let's also come with complete submission to His perfect plan. Only in this can we fulfill the purpose for which we were created. Heavenly Father, we give our life fully into Your hands - let it unfold, not by our plans, goals or desires, but according to Your will.

FINISH THE RACE

Paul was returning to Jerusalem at the end of his third and final missionary journey. By this time in his ministry, Paul had been a Christian for nearly twenty years. Twenty years since Jesus called Paul, "My chosen instrument to carry My name before the Gentiles and their kings and before the people of Israel" (Acts 9:15). Twenty years of faithful service, and now... "In every city the Holy Spirit warns me that prison and hardships are facing me" (Acts 20:23).

Paul was returning home, but his life was not going to be easy. He knew there were many trials ahead, but his life had a purpose far beyond his immediate surroundings.

Acts 20:24

> *"I consider my life worth nothing to me, if only I may finish the race and complete the task the Lord Jesus has given me - the task of testifying to the gospel of God's grace."*

It was several more years before Paul wrote; "I have learned the secret of being content in any and every situation" (Philippians 4:12); yet here, when facing certain hardship, Paul showed he had already learned the secret. The particular circumstances in Paul's life had become of minor importance. He knew his contentment was not based on current events, but on bringing glory and honor to God. His life had a wonderful purpose even in the face of great adversity and harsh conditions.

We were all created for the same purpose as Paul - we were created to bring glory and honor to God! Our specific tasks may differ and change from time to time, but we each have the same unchanging purpose - everything we do, say, and think should bring glory and honor to our Heavenly Father!

God's race is run in the deepest part of our heart - not in the flurry of activity. Running well is not defined by doing more; rather, we run a "successful" race as we do every little task we are given with the complete and absolute devotion of our heart.

His race is long and often difficult. There are many distractions which seek to slow us down and even pull us from the track, and at times we may even wonder why we're running. But being a participant in God's eternal race is infinitely more rewarding than standing on the sidelines and simply watching! He has called us to run - and to run well!!

We must run the path God places before us with all the strength He provides - and within the sure and calming protection of His grace. Let's run with the motivation of bringing Him glory and honor by loving Him with ALL our heart, soul, mind, and strength. Let's continue to run well, and with a burning desire to finish the race.

WHO TAUGHT US TO WALK

In the message "Finish The Race" we were encouraged to "run" toward the finish line; but we were also reminded that God's race takes place within our heart as we learn to trust and love Him more and more. His race is not in what we do, but in who we are and who we are becoming as we do ALL to bring Him glory and honor. One of the biggest stumbling blocks which keeps us from running a "successful" race is the complacency caused by forgetting what God has already done in our life.

Not everyone's circumstances are what they might prefer, but each of us are on a wonderful journey which began when God sent His Spirit to open our eyes to the truth and called us to be with Him for all eternity through faith in His Son. Our beginning ought to be a clear indication of God's miraculous grace and Guiding Hand. And as we look back on our journey, we can recognize some of the miracles which brought us to where we are today. But many we fail to acknowledge or understand - and most we have simply forgotten.

God's children have always had a hard time with recognizing and remembering. The northern kingdom of Israel had been in rebellion for almost two hundred years when God called Hosea to be a prophet. The people had created their own form of worship and had long forgotten how much God loved them and how much He had already done to guide and protect.

Hosea 11:3-4

"It was I {God} who taught Ephraim to walk, taking them by the arms; but they did not realize it was I who healed them. I led them with cords of human kindness, with ties of love; I lifted the yoke from their neck and bent down to feed them."

In this passage, Ephraim refers to the nation of Israel. God was reminding the people how He provided for all their needs as He led them out of Egyptian slavery, into the promised land of Canaan. But this passage is very applicable to each of us today. Whether we see His Hand or not, God has been at work guiding us in many different ways.

None of us are at our final destination, but each of us are where we are because God loves us dearly and wants to draw us ever closer to Himself. Let's not create our own form of worship where we give Him the leftovers of our heart. He created us, saved us, and brought us to where we are today - He deserves our ALL.

We must turn our eyes back to God and praise Him for His continuous provision and His loving promise to finish the work He has begun in our life; "He who began a good work in you will carry it on to completion" (Philippians 1:6). Let's praise Him for His Guiding Hand, and, as we run, let's always remember it was God who taught us to walk.

A DARKENED HEART

When God called Jeremiah to be a prophet, the people of Jerusalem had been living in sin for a very long time. It had been 300 years since the kingdom of Israel divided; and despite God's patient warnings, the people continued to rebel and worship other gods.

God finally told Jeremiah He would no longer endure this continued rejection; "I have withdrawn My blessing, My love and My pity from this people" (Jeremiah 16:5). God also said that because of the many years of rebellion, destruction was now certain; "I will bring an end to the sounds of joy and gladness" (Jeremiah 16:9). He then told Jeremiah how to respond to the inevitable cries and complaints.

Jeremiah 16:10-12

"When you tell these people all this and they ask you, 'Why has the Lord decreed such a great disaster against us? What wrong have we done? What sin have we committed against the Lord our God?' then say to them, 'It is because your fathers forsook Me,' declares the Lord, 'and followed other gods and served and worshiped them. They forsook Me and did not keep My law. But you have behaved more wickedly than your fathers.'"

This is a difficult message. God is characterized by extreme grace and patient love...but He has His limits. He will not tolerate continual disobedience. If we claim to be a child of God we must deal with the very real issue of sin. God hates sin because it causes separation with those He loves.

Continual and unrepented sin causes us to lose the ability to recognize our sin. It becomes a cancer which causes our heart to turn cold and dark, unable to even hear the conviction of the Holy Spirit; "For although they knew God, they neither glorified Him as God nor gave thanks to Him, but their thinking became futile and their foolish hearts were darkened" (Romans 1:21). Sin clouds our vision and causes us to drift further and further from God's path.

The people of Jerusalem could no longer recognize their sin - they stood before God in their wickedness and boldly asked: "What wrong have we done?" Today, we are at risk of becoming equally darkened anytime we fail to address the sin which continues to push into our lives. What activities have we begun to tolerate? What behaviors have we begun to accept? What "teachings" from the modern media have we begun to receive? What sin has begun to fill our heart?

If our eyes were truly opened, would we be surprised to see how far we've compromised and strayed? Let's recommit our lives to holiness, purity, worship, and absolute love for God. Let's allow His light to indwell EVERY area of our life. Let's repent of our sin and refuse to live with a darkened heart.

AN UNKNOWN GOD

When Paul was on his second missionary journey, he came to the city of Athens which was inhabited by people who loved to worship and talk about their worship. They worshipped every conceivable god of their day and made sure no god was left out.

Acts 17:22-23

"Paul then stood up in the meeting of the Areopagus and said: 'Men of Athens! I see that in every way you are very religious. For as I walked around and looked carefully at your objects of worship, I even found an altar with this inscription: TO AN UNKNOWN GOD. Now what you worship as something unknown I am going to proclaim to you.'"

The people in Athens worshipped gods like Zeus, Hermes, and Diana. And to ensure they did not overlook any god, they also gave their worship to a god they did not know.

Today, many of us go through our life worshipping such gods as Pleasure, Leisure, Entertainment, Security, Power, and Wealth. Then, usually with much less intensity and commitment, we "worship" the Creator of the Universe. But our worship often becomes something we schedule and not something we live. We take part in religious activity, but have no idea how to make the Almighty God an integral part of our everyday life. We attend church services, but never give a thought to actually loving God or asking Him for guidance and direction. We go through the motions of worship, but our hearts are cold and far from the One True God.

We ALL must examine what we believe, and then live a life consistent with that belief. Many people profess belief in God - even the God of the Bible - but have no idea what this belief means or Who they really believe. They believe and then attempt to worship, a God they do not know. If Christ died for the forgiveness of our sins, was resurrected, and now sits at the right hand of the Father making intercession on our behalf - if He will one day return and take us to be with Him for all eternity - then He certainly deserves more than our casual worship and the left-overs of our time.

Our Heavenly Father has been calling us back to an intimate fellowship ever since Adam and Eve sinned in the garden; and His message has remained the same: 'Enjoy My creation, but give Me ALL your heart.' He must be given sole possession, without any competition. The true Creator of the Universe will never accept just being one of our many "gods."

Let's proclaim the absolute and unchanging truth and encourage one another to "wholeheartedly obey the form of teaching to which you were entrusted" (Romans 6:17). Let's resolve to live a consistent life - a life of sincere love and faithful service - a life which no longer worships an unknown God.

COVENANT OF WORSHIP

In the message "An Unknown God" we were encouraged to live a life of sincere love and faithful service while we worship a God we truly know and adore. But this type of consistent life, where our daily activities match what we profess to believe, does not come easy or initially feel natural; it requires a firm commitment and a determined perseverance.

King Asa was the great-grandson of Solomon and led the southern kingdom of Judah about 900 years before Christ. He began his reign with ten years of peace because he "did what was right in the eyes of the Lord his God" (2 Chronicles 14:2). Asa took definite action to remove the idols and places of false worship from the country and commanded his people to "seek the Lord and to obey His commands" (2 Chronicles 14:4).

When Judah was invaded by a foreign army, Asa realized he was greatly outnumbered with little hope of victory. As he went into battle, his faith was strengthened while calling on God: "Help us, O Lord our God, for we rely on You, and in Your name we have come against this vast army. O Lord, You are our God; do not let man prevail against You" (2 Chronicles 14:11).

After God granted them victory on the battlefield, the people gathered in Jerusalem to solidify their commitment by making a covenant to follow God.

2 Chronicles 15:12,15

"They entered into a covenant to seek the Lord with all their heart and soul. All Judah rejoiced about the oath because they had sworn it wholeheartedly. They sought God eagerly, and He was found by them."

Every child of God has a deep desire for a more committed life. When we have answered God's call and begun our journey with Him, we will not be at peace until His praise fills every area of our life. But this requires we establish priorities which allow us to actually spend time getting to know Him - His ways and His love.

Our Heavenly Father longs for us to abide in His presence; He rejoices when He is found by those who seek Him in a committed life of worship. He even promises to help those who begin down a committed path; "For the eyes of the Lord range throughout the earth to strengthen those whose hearts are fully committed to Him" (2 Chronicles 16:9).

Our time on this earth is very, very short. Let's not waste another day by aimlessly wandering through life - by allowing the concerns of this world to choke off our relationship with God. Let's live with purpose and eagerly commit to seek Him with all our heart and soul - to seek Him "wholeheartedly." Let's make the decision today to enter into an eternal covenant of worship.

A BROKEN COVENANT

In the message "A Covenant of Worship" we were encouraged to make a covenant to love the Lord and worship Him with all our heart. This covenant must be viewed as a pledge or binding agreement which directs all our actions. God gives many examples of covenants in His Word; and no where does He allow for a covenant with half-hearted commitment.

When God brought the Israelites out of Egypt, He made a covenant with them at Mount Sinai. He promised special blessings if they would set themselves apart and worship Him with all their heart. But the people failed to honor their commitment - they worshiped other gods and disregarded His Commands.

After several hundred years of willful disobedience, God sent the prophet Hosea to remind them of the pledge they once made and to reveal their unfaithfulness.

Hosea 6:6-7

"I desire mercy, not sacrifice, and acknowledgment of God rather than burnt offerings. Like Adam, they have broken the covenant - they were unfaithful to Me."

Hosea was able to deliver this message with great passion because he understood the pain of unfaithfulness. God had called him to marry a woman who, though she made a covenant of marriage, left him to live as an adulteress with another man. He could literally cry to his Israelite Brothers of the hurt they were causing God with their Spiritual adultery; he fully knew how it felt when the one you love turns away to love another.

The covenant we make with our Heavenly Father must not be taken lightly. He loves us dearly and gave His Son as a sacrifice for our sin; and to those who believe, He has given His Spirit, "with whom you were sealed for the day of redemption" (Ephesians 4:30). He is committed to this covenant; and, though He forgives us when we fall short, He expects and deserves commitment in return.

When we turn from sin and believe Jesus to be our Lord and Savior, He promises forgiveness - we promise to trust and follow where He leads. He promises a clean heart, we promise our heart will always be His. He promises eternity in His presence, we promise to worship Him with every breath!

Have we truly entered into a covenant relationship with the Living God? And if so, are we being faithful to this covenant? Are we seeking His direction, or are we following our own path and our own desires? We must commit to love, honor, cherish...and follow, until the end of this life brings us fully into His presence. Let's remain faithful and true to our promises. Let's renew our commitment to obedience and worship, and refuse to come to the end of this journey with a broken covenant.

CONTINUE TO SEEK

As Jesus was speaking to a Pharisee named Nicodemus, He said, "no one can see the Kingdom of God unless he is born again" (John 3:3). He then explained being "born again" as a Spiritual birth which occurs when we believe; "whoever believes in Him shall not perish but have eternal life" (John 3:16). EVERYONE who will spend eternity in the Presence of God must be born of the Spirit - it is impossible to be a Child of God without being "born again."

This Spiritual birth is part of the New Covenant through faith in Jesus and was revealed over 500 years before Christ through the prophet Ezekiel; "I will remove from you your heart of stone and give you a heart of flesh. And I will put My Spirit in you and move you to follow my decrees" (Ezekiel 36:26-27). Paul refers to the Spiritual birth as becoming "a new creation" (2 Corinthians 5:17), but it is most often referred to simply as being saved; "He saved us through the washing of rebirth and renewal by the Holy Spirit" (Titus 3:5).

The process of Spiritual birth is relatively easy to explain - God reaches down and transforms our heart by the power of His Spirit. However, the exact events which lead to the Spiritual birth (and when the birth actually occurs) remain somewhat a mystery. On one

65

hand, God's Word is very simple and clear; "Whoever believes will be saved." But understanding what it means to really believe can be difficult. We can talk about submission, obedience, sacrifice, love, or the basic faith of a child, but these will always fall short of an adequate definition of belief.

Only God can save; only He is fit to judge; and He alone can look into the innermost part of our heart and determine true belief. All we can do is seek Him with all our heart - and trust He will be found.

Matthew 7:7-8

"Ask and it will be given to you; seek and you will find; knock and the door will be opened to you. For everyone who asks receives; he who seeks finds; and to him who knocks, the door will be opened."

Our Salvation was initiated by God when Jesus came to earth and died as a perfect sacrifice for our sin. He chose us for an intimate and eternal relationship when His Holy Spirit began to call us near. And, if we will but answer the call and begin to seek His face, He will be found. In an instant, which He alone determines according to His perfect timing, He will transform our heart and adopt us as His Child.

We may not be able to explain or even fully understand true belief, but if there is any call of God on our heart we CAN ask, seek, and knock. God never hides nor runs away; "He is not far from each one of us" (Acts 17:27). He is waiting for us to reach out and call on His Name. Today, let's trust He will be found as we give Him all our heart and continue to seek.

GUARD THE GOOD DEPOSIT

In the messages "Covenant of Worship" and "A Broken Covenant" we were encouraged to make a covenant - which we resolve not to break - to worship God with all our heart for the rest of our days. I pray we accept this challenge and make a decision to commit our lives to Him without any reservation.

When God brings us to this point of greater commitment and surrender, we have a wonderful reason to rejoice; but we also have an obligation to protect and nurture what He has planted in our heart. He has called us to draw closer and spend more time in His presence - to join Him in a more intimate and loving relationship - but the enemy is hard at work trying to destroy the change which has begun.

2 Timothy 1:13-14

"What you heard from me, keep as the pattern of sound teaching, with faith and love in Christ Jesus. Guard the good deposit that was entrusted to you - guard it with the help of the Holy Spirit who lives in us."

Every so often on our Christian walk, there comes a time of special closeness with God. This closeness may come as the result of a new understanding of His Word where we see His character like never before. It may come during a solitary time of prayer or while worshiping with many other believers, through a powerful speaker or inspirational writing. Each time this occurs, God is depositing a little truth into our life which says: I am the way, draw nearer and follow Me more.

We know when God calls us in this manner. We know His truth; we know He is lighting the only true way, and we honestly desire to follow. But then we're back at work with deadlines to meet, people to see, or kids to feed. Soon, the busyness of our everyday "normal" life has consumed our thoughts, and God's deposit has begun to fade - this should not be!

We must establish disciplines which enable us to hear God's message and then help us keep His message at the forefront of our thoughts all through the day. These disciplines will vary for different people. Some may need to wake up earlier to have a time which is quiet; others may need to change their work habits or the condition of their work environment. But we all, regardless of our hectic pace, need to simply talk with God more and worship more at His feet. This must become our highest priority.

We cannot allow His gifts to be destroyed or forgotten. We should never allow the frustrations of the past, the pulls of the present or the desires of the future, to steal the gifts entrusted to us today. Let's make the necessary changes and boldly draw near without hesitation. Let's praise Him for His gifts, and, "with the help of the Holy Spirit who lives in us," guard the good deposit.

HOW TO GUARD HIS DEPOSIT

In the message "Guard The Good Deposit" we saw the importance of protecting what God places on our heart. He often gives us moments of Divine intimacy as a taste of the life He desires for us - a life of continual passion for God; a life where all our thoughts, words, and deeds become an act of worship.

As these moments fade, we either take definite steps and choose to follow God's call, or we allow our heart to slowly drift away. The world will naturally pull us from God's desire and cause us to forget He has even called. So how do we really "guard" what God has given and truly accept His invitation to draw near?

Deuteronomy 11:17-20

"Fix these words of Mine in your hearts and minds; tie them as symbols on your hands and bind them on your foreheads. Teach them to your children, talking about them when you sit at home and when you walk along the road, when you lie down and when you get up. Write them on the doorframes of your houses and on your gate."

When God called the children of Israel, He knew they would face the same difficulties we face today: "Be careful, or you will be enticed to turn away and worship other gods and bow down to them" (Deuteronomy 11:16). He said the values of the world must never distract from our primary duty to "love the Lord your God with all your heart and with all your soul and with all your strength" (Deuteronomy 6:5).

God told His chosen people the best way to remain near to Him was to remain near to His Word through disciplined reading, teaching, discussing, and applying. When our lives are completely immersed in His Word, the "enticements" of the world lose their power and no longer pull us from God's path.

But His desire was never for us to stop with outward disciplines. While they are somewhat useful in themselves, the desired end is always for His Word to be written on our heart and for our thoughts to remain with Him all through our day! Only as He is allowed to truly live through us will our lives become a complete sacrifice of worship.

If this is the life we desire, then we must begin with a disciplined approach to God's Word. I suggest we set aside a specific time and place each day which we can completely devote to prayer and the quiet study of ALL His Word. He will soon reward us with a more intimate relationship as His Word becomes written on our heart. As we continue to grow, our thoughts will turn more and more to Christ. What began as great effort will soon become as natural as breathing. The world will still try to pull us away, but it will no longer succeed; for we will be walking in His Presence and will have learned how to guard His deposit.

FREE IN THE FIRE

King Nebuchadnezzar had made a large statue of gold and commanded that everyone must worship the statue whenever they heard the sound of music - they must worship the statue, or face terrible consequences! "Whoever does not fall down and worship will immediately be thrown into a blazing furnace" (Daniel 3:6).

Daniel's friends, Shadrach, Meshach, and Abednego, were determined to live with an uncompromising faith. They believed God's Word and obeyed His commands: "You shall have no other gods before Me...you shall not bow down to them or worship them" (Exodus 20:3,5). These three young Jewish men took a stand and refused to worship the golden statue. Their devotion to God was greater than their fear of the fire; "If we are thrown into the blazing furnace, the God we serve is able to save us from it...But even if He does not, we will not serve your gods or worship the image of gold you have set up" (Daniel 3:17-18).

Nebuchadnezzar was furious and followed through on his threat: "He ordered the furnace heated seven times hotter than usual and commanded some of the strongest soldiers in his army to tie up Shadrach, Meshach and Abednego and throw them into the blazing furnace" (Daniel 3:19-20). But when Nebuchadnezzar looked inside the furnace, he was amazed by what he saw.

Daniel 3:25

"Look! I see four men walking around in the fire, unbound and unharmed, and the fourth looks like a son of the gods."

As they were facing the fire, Shadrach, Meshach, and Abednego saw no chance of escape, but they placed their complete trust in God - a trust which would not falter even if they were burned. But rather than being burned by the fire, these three men were freed from their binding ropes and walked with "a son of the gods," who many believe is an Old Testament reference to Jesus Christ! (The KJV renders this verse "...like the Son of God"). In their time of greatest need, God comforted these young men and set them free.

The fires in our life WILL come. The heat will seem intense, but we must not fear or abandon what we know to be true. Our faith is ALWAYS refined and made stronger by fire; "the testing of your faith develops perseverance" (James 1:3). Fire will always teach us to trust more deeply and worship more sincerely. When we really believe this truth, it will become possible to actually rejoice in the face of fire because we KNOW He is in complete and absolute control over every area of our life - this is true freedom! Let's walk with a bold faith, knowing our Father is there to comfort and protect us, knowing He will strengthen us and set us free in the fire.

BE PREPARED TO FOLLOW

We are often reminded of our need to pray and study God's Word. These essential disciplines allow us to abide in the presence of God and "hear" when He calls; they are also necessary for strengthening our faith in order to obediently follow where He leads.

God's Word encourages us that when He calls, He also provides the tools to accomplish our assigned task; "His divine power has given us everything we need for life and godliness" (2 Peter 1:3). We are also comforted that as we respond, we will never be alone; "Never will I leave you; never will I forsake you" (Hebrews 13:5). But God's call also carries responsibility; His call says He has made His choice - He has chosen us to take part in His wonderful plan, and, in faith, we must respond.

After delivering many of God's messages to the people of Israel - calling them to repent and return to the worship of the One True God - the prophet Jeremiah became impatient with God's timing: "I would speak with You about Your justice: Why does the way of the wicked prosper? Why do all the faithless live at ease?" (Jeremiah 12:1). Jeremiah complained about how long he had to wait for the wicked to be punished. He was following God and calling others to do the same, but the ungodly seemed to continue living the "good" life - sounds like our complaints today. But God's response wasn't what Jeremiah was hoping to receive.

Jeremiah 12:5

"If you have raced with men on foot and they have worn you out, how can you compete with horses? If you stumble in safe country, how will you manage in the thickets by the Jordan?"

God told Jeremiah that the situation in Israel was going to get worse in the coming days; He asked Jeremiah if he was truly ready for the challenge. Jeremiah had been called to be God's messenger and now was not the time to complain - this was the time to be a soldier and trust with ALL his heart; it was a time to renew his strength, and push toward the assigned goal.

Our Heavenly Father dearly loves us and desires an eternity of intimate fellowship. He is a God of great comfort, but He is also our Commanding Officer who challenges us to prepare for the Spiritual battles ahead. As bad and unjust as things often appears, the condition of the world will probably become much worse. We must trust now more than ever that God chose the right person when He gave us our assignments; He has made His call and promised to provide all the necessary tools at the proper time.

Let's spend more time worshipping at His feet and loving Him with all our heart. Let's rely on His strength and trust His understanding - let's draw closer to His side and always be prepared to follow.

STRONG IN HIS GRACE

When we are brought to the point of belief - the point where we see our sin, desire to change, and acknowledge God's Son as our only way to Heaven - we ask, in faith, for Jesus to forgive our sins and be our Savior. At that very moment, the grace of God abounds, His Spirit transforms our heart and He picks us up as His child: "For it is by grace you have been saved, through faith - and this not from yourselves, it is the gift of God - not by works, so that no one can boast" (Ephesians 2:8-9).

The moment of true Salvation is without question the most significant event in our Christian life. In that moment, we are "born again" (John 3:7) and become a "new creation" in Christ (2 Corinthians 5:17) through the power of the Holy Spirit; "Flesh gives birth to flesh, but the Spirit gives birth to spirit" (John 3:6). In fact, the moment of Salvation is so significant that even if we seem to stumble through every step past that point, we still have reason to rejoice with every breath - we are children of the King and will spend all eternity in His glorious Kingdom.

As we continue on this sometimes rocky journey, we are to strive for holiness and purposeful worship in our life. We are to diligently seek Him and "learn the secret of being content in any and every situation" (Philippians 4:12). We must learn to "trust in the Lord with all our heart" (Proverbs 3:5), but we must also remember that "apart from Me {Jesus}, you can do NOTHING" (John 15:5). If we strive in our own strength, we are all destined to fall.

2 Timothy 2:1

"You then, my son, be strong in the grace that is in Christ Jesus."

This means we must continue to trust in His grace and in His grace alone. We did nothing to earn our Salvation and we can do nothing to maintain our right standing before God, besides believing in His Son; "Are you so foolish? After beginning with the Spirit, are you now trying to attain your goal by human effort?" (Galatians 3:3).

We are saved by the grace of God and we must continue to live by this same grace: "So then, just as you received Christ Jesus as Lord, continue to live in Him, rooted and built up in Him, strengthened in the faith as you were taught" (Colossians 2:6). Our Heavenly Father will determine our path to holiness, purpose, contentment, and trust - and His grace will equip us with all we need for the journey.

Let's completely trust in the saving grace of Jesus! Let's apply the strength of His grace today in every trial and temptation. Let's live a life of pure and holy devotion by always remaining strong in His grace.

HIS AMAZING GRACE

In the message "Strong In His Grace" we considered God's grace in the process of Salvation and saw we can do nothing to earn a right standing in His eyes. Our Heavenly Father poured out His love when He gave us Jesus; "But God demonstrates His own love for us in this: While we were still sinners, Christ died for us" (Romans 5:8).

God, through His amazing grace, gave us His Son and said, "Whoever believes in Him shall not perish but have eternal life" (John 3:16). We are allowed into an eternal relationship with God because of His grace and are strongly exhorted to live each day knowing our relationship is maintained by the same grace in which it began, not by anything we do or accomplish.

There are many things we are called to do as a Child of God, many ways to serve and honor our Heavenly Father, many ways to be obedient and seek after holiness; but we can NEVER fall into the trap of thinking, even for a moment, that what we do adds to our Salvation by grace. As much as faith in Jesus Christ is absolutely necessary for our Salvation, faith in Jesus Christ is also absolutely sufficient.

Paul delivered this message in many of his letters, but no where as strong as in his letter to the Galatian churches. He had preached the message of Salvation by grace, but they had been led into a false teaching which said they must earn their Salvation by first submitting to the Old Testament Law. Paul warned that if we fall into this same trap, "Christ will be of no value to you at all" (Galatians 5:2). The things we do have value, but the value is not in the religious activity or product we produce; rather, the only thing God will recognize is the faith in our heart which ought to motivate ALL we seek to accomplish.

Galatians 5:6
"The only thing that counts is faith expressing itself through love."

We show our love for God through worship, thanksgiving, prayer, study, obedience, and faithful service; and we acknowledge His saving grace with a humble spirit which does not allow us to become puffed up or feel deserving of our Salvation. We demonstrate our love for others as we refuse to cause harm, in word or deed, refuse to harbor unforgiveness, and actively look for opportunities to serve. And we show an understanding of God's grace as we express our love without requiring others to earn our love or even love us in return.

Let's receive His grace with a thankful heart, knowing we bring nothing to the cross besides our sin which He then takes away. Let's trust only in His grace, given to us through faith, and express our faith with all our heart, soul, mind, and strength as we love Him and love one another. Let's begin to live this life like we truly understand His amazing grace.

GRACE IN OTHERS

In the last two messages, we've considered the grace of God in our Salvation as well as in our daily Christian walk. Anytime we add requirements to faith, we have strayed from the true gospel message. We certainly need to be challenged as to what faith really means and how a saving faith will manifest itself in our life, but we must never walk away from Salvation by grace through faith alone.

Galatians 1:6-8

"I am astonished that you are so quickly deserting the one who called you by the grace of Christ and are turning to a different gospel - which is really no gospel at all. Evidently some people are throwing you into confusion and are trying to pervert the gospel of Christ. But even if we or an angel from heaven should preach a gospel other than the one we preached to you, let him be eternally condemned!"

This is a serious call - one we cannot ignore. We are challenged in the strongest of terms to continue walking according to the true gospel.

We usually begin this walk by focusing on our own life. We slowly take our eyes off of what we can do and look more upon what Christ has already done; "He must become greater, I must become less" (John 3:30). But there remains another step we must begin to take. This important step is to recognize that the grace which pulled us out of the slimy pit and set our feet on solid ground (Psalm 40:2) is the same grace which works in the life of others. We know we can do nothing to earn or add to our Salvation, but how often do we place "requirements" on those around us?

As an example: In some churches the men always wear a necktie and have difficulty with those who professes to love the Lord but fail to conform to the "Law of the Necktie." Likewise, in other churches people worship in shorts and tee shirts. And likewise, though they preach Salvation by grace through faith, they have difficulty with those who professes to love the Lord but come to worship more dressed up and do not conform to the "Freedom" we have in Christ. Both groups look at the other and say, "How can they really be saved dressed like that?"

This may seem like a trivial example, but I trust the Spirit will guide as to how this applies in your own life. How about things like hair style or worship style? How about those "sins" which we, in our great wisdom, have identified as indications of true Salvation but which the Bible remains absolutely silent?

We must strive to follow Christ in a surrendered obedience; but, in doing so, we must never pull anyone from the true gospel. We are saved by grace through faith and faith alone - and "we" includes ALL our Brothers and Sisters. Let's follow hard in His grace and diligently seek to recognize God's grace in others.

SPIRITUAL WISDOM AND UNDERSTANDING

Paul wrote his letter to the Colossians to show that Jesus is sufficient to supply every need of the believer. In the opening verses, Paul wrote that the Colossians had a reputation for great faith in Jesus Christ - their love, hope, and hunger for the Gospel was bearing fruit and had been growing "since the day you heard it and understood God's grace" (Colossians 1:6).

Paul was thankful for their strong faith, but he wanted them to have even more and was committed to praying for their continued growth; "We have not stopped praying for you and asking God to fill you with the knowledge of His will through all Spiritual wisdom and understanding" (Colossians 1:9).

Paul then explained the purpose of his prayer.

Colossians 1:10-12

"We pray this in order that you may live a life worthy of the Lord and may please Him in every way: bearing fruit in every good work, growing in the knowledge of God, being strengthened with all power according to His glorious might so that you may have great endurance and

patience, and joyfully giving thanks to the Father."

Though God's gracious gift of Salvation is free, the cost is high. We can do nothing to earn or maintain this gift besides believe in His Son; but the faith through which His grace flows is a faith committed to Him without reservation - prepared to follow anywhere He leads and willing to honor Him in all we do.

Paul didn't pray for the details of an honoring life; rather, he prayed for what truly produces change; "the knowledge of His will through all Spiritual wisdom and understanding." We never please God by focusing on specific activities, we please Him by drawing near and allowing His blessings to flow in and through our life. This is a life which bears fruit and is filled with endurance, patience, and thankfulness.

This life is available for us today...regardless of our circumstances. But we must draw nearer to our Heavenly Father and hunger for a better understanding of His will. We must long for His presence and continue to grow in love and faith. God has infinitely more to give and will only pour His blessings upon those who continue to seek Him with all their heart.

Dear Lord, we pray that You will give us a continued passion for You and an increased hunger for Your Word. We pray that You will strengthen our faith and use our life for Your glory. Heavenly Father, we pray that we will abandon ourself to You and that You will fill us with the knowledge of Your will through all Spiritual wisdom and understanding.

NOTHING TOO HARD

Jeremiah had been a prophet for nearly forty years by the time Jerusalem came under attack by the Babylonians. He had long been proclaiming a message of repentance, but the people continued to ignore his words; now the enemy had surrounded Jerusalem and the end was near. In this time of great turmoil, God told Jeremiah to purchase a field from his cousin.

This was a strange request, but Jeremiah obediently purchased the field. However, he soon began to question God's reasoning: "See how the siege ramps are built up to take the city? Though the city will be handed over to the Babylonians, You say to me, 'Buy the field'" (Jeremiah 32:24,25). Jeremiah had been a prophet for many years. He had been given the privilege of talking directly with God, but this command just didn't make sense. Why should he purchase a field when the enemy was invading and taking prisoners?

God answered Jeremiah with a simple, yet challenging question.

Jeremiah 32:27

"I am the Lord, the God of all mankind. Is anything too hard for Me?"

Yes, the enemy had invaded the land and would soon overrun the city of Jerusalem. But God's plan was for the people to one day return: "I will surely gather them from all the lands where I banish them in My furious anger and great wrath; I will bring them back to this place and let them live in safety. They will be My people and I will be their God" (Jeremiah 32:37-38). Jeremiah's field was to be a reminder that God would one day restore His people - a reminder that He could be trusted even in the face of overwhelming circumstances.

We often have a difficult time seeing how all the pieces of God's plan fit together. He leads us down a path and we fail to see the purpose - especially when the enemy begins to attack. We want to fight back, but God says to patiently trust Him and pray; we want to determine a solution and solve the problem, but God says to love Him with all our heart and share His love with others.

The times in which we are most tested and pressed down ought to be the times of greatest growth and closeness with our Heavenly Father. When it seems we have no where else to turn, we ought to rejoice and trust Him even more! Let's put our life firmly in His Hands and submit to His guidance - even when we may not see where we are going or how we will get there. Let's trust His ways and always remember...for God, there is NOTHING too hard!

THE EXAMPLE OF BARNABAS

Prior to meeting Jesus on the road to Damascus, Saul (who would later be known as the Apostle Paul) was one of the greatest enemies of Christians: "Saul began to destroy the church. Going from house to house, he dragged off men and women and put them in prison" (Acts 8:3). But Saul's conversion was dramatic and after a few years he tried to join with the believers in Jerusalem. However, with his reputation for hatred toward Christians, the disciples were not willing to accept him.

But one man saw beyond the past mistakes; saw beyond the slimy pit from which he had been removed; saw the grace of Jesus which had worked a miracle in Saul's life - that man was Barnabas! Barnabas believed in Saul, comforted him, and defended him to the other believers.

Acts 9:27

"But Barnabas took him and brought him to the apostles. He told them how Saul on his journey had seen the Lord and that the Lord had spoken to him, and how in Damascus he had preached fearlessly in the name of Jesus."

Saul was on fire for Jesus, ready to preach the gospel with the same energy he once used to persecute the church. But after just a short time in Jerusalem, Saul had to flee for his life back to his home in Tarsus. It's not clear what he did for the next several years, but there's no evidence of ministry work until Barnabas, once again, found Saul and provided the necessary encouragement.

Acts 11:25-26

"Barnabas went to Tarsus to look for Saul, and when he found him, he brought him to Antioch. So for a whole year Barnabas and Saul met with the church and taught great numbers of people."

The Apostle Paul went on to have a greater impact in the forming of the early Church and in defining Church doctrine than any other follower of Jesus. But if not for Barnabas, Paul may not have ever preached beyond his own back yard. In the early days of the Church, Barnabas believed in the absolute best in people and encouraged them at every opportunity. His encouragement of Paul resulted in more fruit for God's Kingdom than anything else he could have possibly done or imagined.

We all know someone who can use a lift - someone in desperate need of a friend to believe in them - someone in need of a Barnabas! Let's encourage others today by believing in the power of Christ working through their lives; by looking beyond what we can see, to what we know Jesus can do with a life completely devoted to Him. Let's be the spark which reignites the fire in others and helps them return to the great race - let's look for opportunities to encourage our Brothers and Sisters according to the example of Barnabas.

SON OF ENCOURAGEMENT

In the message "The Example of Barnabas" we saw how Barnabas played an essential role in Paul's ministry. He boldly introduced Paul to the apostles in Jerusalem (Acts 9:27), and then searched for Paul when he had fled Jerusalem to his home town of Tarsus (Acts 11:25-26). After taking Paul to Antioch, Barnabas remained with him for several years while they encouraged the church - and each other.

Being an encourager was a way of life for Barnabas. His name was originally Joseph, but, prior to even meeting Paul, the apostles had begun to call him "Barnabas (which means Son of Encouragement)" (Acts 4:36). Barnabas was able to evaluate other people according to their ability in Christ - an ability determined by His strength and not hindered by past failures. This allowed Barnabas to see great potential where others saw only weakness and to encourage when others had given up.

Barnabas went with Paul on his first missionary journey where they jointly proclaimed the name of Jesus wherever they went. Another young man, named Mark, began this first missionary journey but then turned back. This apparent lack of perseverance bothered Paul so much that when he began his second missionary trip he refused to take Mark along.

Acts 15:37-39

"Barnabas wanted to take John, also called Mark, with them, but Paul did not think it wise to take him, because he had deserted them in Pamphylia and had not continued with them in the work. They had such a sharp disagreement that they parted company. Barnabas took Mark and sailed for Cyprus."

Barnabas saw the Christ-given potential in young Mark and encouraged him as he had done with Paul many years before. As a result, Mark matured in his ministry and faithfully continued in his service to Jesus. He ministered along side the Apostle Peter (2 Peter 5:13), was reunited with Paul (Colossians 4:10, Philemon 24), and later wrote the earliest account of the Gospel - the Gospel of Mark.

The early church faced many difficulties - many opportunities for discouragement - but God used Barnabas to strengthen those who had been called to the front lines of battle. We can't all stand up and preach in front of large crowds or travel as missionaries to foreign lands, but we ALL have the ability to encourage those who God places in our path.

The world is full of people crying out for someone to care and believe in them. Individual lives can be changed, families can be restored, entire communities and even nations can be turned toward God, if each of us will encourage others to draw closer to our Heavenly Father, to love Him more, and to trust Him with all their heart. Let's share the love of Jesus and effectively minister by seeing others, and then taking action, as a Son of Encouragement.

INTENTIONAL DISCIPLESHIP

In the last two messages, we've seen how Barnabas was an encouragement in the lives of Paul and Mark. We considered how Barnabas must have seen the "Christ-potential" in others and discipled them at critical seasons of their life.

Discipleship involves prayer, teaching, compassion, commitment, and the ability to lead by a Godly example; but there is also an element of discipleship which is extremely active and intentional. When Barnabas saw how Paul was being rejected in Jerusalem, he "took him and brought him to the apostles" (Acts 9:27). When he may have been concerned that Paul was discouraged; "Barnabas went to Tarsus to look for Paul" (Acts 11:25). And when Mark was facing rejection and almost certain discouragement for future ministry; "Barnabas took Mark and sailed for Cyprus" (Acts 15:39).

Each of these events involved much more than a kind word as Barnabas continued on his own path; they involved evaluating the need, and then making the necessary changes in his own path to help meet the need - they involved being intentional.

There was certainly no better example of how to disciple others than Jesus. During His ministry on earth He was an example to all who saw or heard of Him. He taught large groups and ministered to individuals at every opportunity. But with a specific group of twelve, Jesus gave an extra measure of His time and energy to help them grow closer to God and equip them for future ministry.

Luke 6:12-13

"Jesus went out to a mountainside to pray, and spent the night praying to God. When morning came, He called His disciples to Him and chose twelve of them, whom He also designated apostles."

We ought to do more than encourage when it's convenient; more than live a Godly life and hope others will follow. In Jesus, we are given a wonderful example of choosing, through prayer, individuals whom we intentionally lead closer to God. This is clearly His command when Jesus says, "go and make disciples of all nations" (Matthew 28:19).

I wish I could say it's easy to "go and make disciples," but it's not. Getting schedules and desires to match up seems to get harder all the time, and can often become discouraging. And yet, we must not give up. Jesus showed us the way and commanded us to follow - this is the only true plan for discipleship!

Let's continue to lead through the example of a devoted and holy life and encourage those in need at every opportunity. But let's now take the next step and prayerfully identify those who will receive our special attention for an extended period of time. Let's pour ourself into others and help them grow closer to Jesus through intentional discipleship.

GOD'S PERFECT WILL

Much of our Christian walk seems to involve searching for God's will. We search for His perfect will for our job, home, school, church, and relationships; and we're often frustrated because God seems silent regarding the details of our life. But God is not silent! His Word reveals much of His will, and a large portion of His will for our life today is the same as for every past generation.

1 Thessalonians 5:16-18

"Be joyful always; pray continually; give thanks in all circumstances, for this is God's will for you in Christ Jesus."

We often gloss over such passages, thinking we already understand and ought to search for "deeper" truths. But in God's plan for us to be "conformed to the likeness of His Son" (Romans 8:29) there is no greater challenge to our faith. Do we really believe God is in control? Does our life - our attitude - reflect this belief?

Our Heavenly Father desires us to live each moment with a thankful heart, full of joy - regardless of our circumstances. Why? Because this reveals our trust in a loving God. He wants us to continually commune with Him in prayer and refuse to leave His presence to pursue concerns or pleasures of the world. This portion of God's will has been clearly revealed!

Some are facing situations today which make following this portion of God's will very difficult. They see absolutely no reason for rejoicing and can't understand how God can be directing their path. How is it possible to remain by His side when being pressed down from all directions and when the pulls of the world seem relentless?

We must begin by viewing our life from an eternal perspective rather than the temporary nature of the world; "The world and its desires pass away, but the man who does the will of God lives forever" (1 John 2:17). All our trials will soon be gone (do we really believe this?). God is in control and, in the end, ALL will glorify His name; "In all things God works for the good of those who love Him" (Romans 8:28). As we trust and love Him with all our heart, He works ALL things for the good - no matter how bad our situation may appear or how difficult it may be to understand His plan. He IS in control! This level of trust is what Paul referred to as "the secret of being content" (Philippians 4:12).

There are certainly times when God will give us very specific direction, but perhaps He's waiting until we follow His general will for our life. Let's come before Him today with a thankful and loving heart. Let's enter His presence and refuse to be taken away by circumstances which will soon fade. Let's trust Him without compromise and joyfully walk each step by faith according to God's perfect will.

ACTIVELY WAIT

In the message "God's Perfect Will" we saw that God's will is for us to live a life of thanksgiving and prayer; a life of contentment and peace independent of circumstances. It is also "God's will that you should be sanctified {set apart, made holy}; that you should avoid sexual immorality" (1 Thessalonians 4:3). These are general aspects of God's will, given to every one of His Children. His specific direction will come as we obediently align our life with His general will...and wait.

We live in a generation where waiting is viewed as a waste of time, but learning to wait is how we grow: "They that wait upon the Lord shall renew their strength; they shall mount up with wings as eagles; they shall run, and not be weary; and they shall walk, and not faint" (Isaiah 40:31 KJV).

This is a powerful and encouraging passage: if we wait on the Lord, we will be strengthened, soar like the eagles, and not grow weary. But what does it really mean to wait? We were not called to "take up the cross of Salvation" so we can then live our lives sitting on the couch. Rather, as believers in Jesus Christ, we have been invited to a wonderful lifetime journey - a journey which is sometimes difficult, but one always filled with adventure and purpose.

1 Timothy 6:11-12

"But you, man of God, flee from all this {evil}, and pursue righteousness, godliness, faith, love, endurance and gentleness. Fight the good fight of the faith. Take hold of the eternal life to which you were called when you made your good confession in the presence of many witnesses."

Notice all the words of action: flee, pursue, fight, take hold. This is definitely a call to actively move forward in our journey of faith.

So: do we wait, or do we fight and take hold? Do we rest and hope in the Lord, or do we flee and pursue? The answer is simply....yes! We are called to a life of action - to a life where we "bear much fruit" (John 15:8) - but we must learn to "act" while waiting and trusting God for every result. We must give Him all our effort while remaining "in the vine" (John 15:4), and allowing the life of Christ to flow through us and produce the fruit.

This means we are to boldly share the gospel message, but then to wait on God for the harvest of belief. It means we are to seek opportunities and diligently prepare for service, but then continue to listen and trust Him to reveal His desired path.

God calls us to a faith of complete trust; a faith which produces both action and patience. Let's take hold and fight the good fight of faith as we learn to actively wait.

BY ALL POSSIBLE MEANS

The Apostle Paul was a pillar of strength who saw the ways of God more clearly than any other individual. He had a unique boldness in his message because he had received the gospel directly from God: "The gospel I preached is not something that man made up. I did not receive it from any man, nor was I taught it; rather, I received it by revelation from Jesus Christ" (Galatians 1:11-12).

There is no doubt that Paul had a special blessing from God: "This man {Paul} is My chosen instrument to carry My name before the Gentiles and their kings and before the people of Israel" (Acts 9:15). But if Paul would have remained attached to this highly favored position of strength and superior knowledge, his ministry would have been severely limited.

1 Corinthians 9:22

"To the weak I became weak, to win the weak. I have become all things to all men so that by all possible means I might save some."

Paul was so devoted to preaching the Gospel that he could humbly minister to anyone! He was determined to reach every person God placed in his path - even if this meant lowering himself and becoming weak.

We must be careful to understand that weakness does not mean we engage in sin! God NEVER asks us to violate His commands in order to accomplish His will; we never need to sin in order to reach someone with the gospel. Rather, becoming weak means showing compassion without regard to a person's status; it means having the "strength" to walk beside the weak and minister the love of Jesus without condemnation. Godly weakness means showing grace to others because we understand the grace we've been given.

As we minister to the lost - as we touch those without Christ - there must be a single purpose to our message. Without Jesus we are ALL lost and on our way to an eternal damnation; "For all have sinned and fall short of the glory of God" (Romans 3:23). We must never forget this basic truth. We must never let our position in Christ cloud the message of the cross. We have been saved and set free; "He has rescued us from the dominion of darkness" (Colossians 1:13). But now, the world around us is in desperate need of this same Savior.

We each have a message to share - a message which can encourage and be used to draw others to faith in Jesus. Let's begin to share this message with ALL. Let's begin to step outside our select and "comfortable" group - outside the group we relate to and claim to understand. The Good News of Jesus is a precious life-saving gift! Let's begin to share this gift with ALL - by ALL possible means.

PREACH THE WORD

In the message "By All Possible Means" we ended with an encouragement that "we each have a message to share - a message which can encourage and be used to draw others to faith in Jesus." We were then exhorted to "begin to share this message with ALL." But as we boldly go out and begin to minister to others, we must ensure we are ministering according to truth.

Paul's second letter to Timothy was the last of his writings. Written while in prison and awaiting a certain death, Paul used this letter to give some final encouragement to a young preacher.

2 Timothy 4:1-2

"I give you this charge: Preach the Word; be prepared in season and out of season; correct, rebuke and encourage - with great patience and careful instruction."

Paul knew his time of ministry had come to an end - and with his last words, he told Timothy to carefully "Preach the Word." Timothy had been taught the true Word of God, but Paul warned that people would not accept this truth; "Instead, to suit their own desires, they will gather around them a great number of teachers to say what their itching ears want to hear" (2 Timothy 4:3).

There have always been those who distort the Gospel message - always those who remove the sufficiency of the Cross or the necessity of a repentant heart. The world rewards those who dilute the truth of Christ with the philosophy of man and his methods of success. Unfortunately, false teachers will continue to abound and will always have an audience.

But we must refuse to compromise! We have been given the Word of God - a message of truth. And while this message is a wonderful blessing, it also carries an incredible responsibility. We are called to know this message and apply its principles of forgiveness, grace, and love as we live a life devoted to holiness, thanksgiving, and praise. We then must share this message of absolute truth with others at every opportunity.

Our time here is very, very short. We are "a mist that appears for a little while and then vanishes" (James 4:14). Some of us may vanish in a few days, others not for many years - but we will ALL vanish. What remains in the end will ONLY be that which is done according to truth and for the glory of God.

Let's focus more of our time and effort on the treasures which last for eternity. Let's remain aligned to His Word and continue to apply the truth we have received; sharing with others, without shame or compromise. Let's accept the charge today to stand firm and Preach the Word!

THE NAME OF JESUS

In the message "Preach The Word" we were strongly encouraged to share a message of truth with the world which is uncompromising and aligned with the Word of God. We cannot continue to trust in the messages of the world, nor in the teaching of the "religious" when their words are not supported by Biblical Truth!

Toward the end of a passage we call "The Sermon on the Mount," Jesus gave a strong warning: "Enter through the narrow gate. For wide is the gate and broad is the road that leads to destruction, and many enter through it. But small is the gate and narrow the road that leads to life, and only a few find it" (Matthew 7:13-14). Our message must always lead down the "narrow road" and toward the "narrow gate" of Salvation. If it does, it is truth and honoring to God; if it does not, it is full of deceit and grieves our Heavenly Father.

Of course, the most important aspect of a true message is the name of Jesus. If our message does not include the sacrifice of Jesus as our necessary AND sufficient path to forgiveness and eternal life, then we do not carry a message of truth. Without Jesus there is no Christian faith - there is no eternal hope.

Philippians 2:9-11

"Therefore God exalted Him to the highest place and gave Him the name that is above every name, that at the name of Jesus every knee should bow, in Heaven and on earth and under the earth, and every tongue confess that Jesus Christ is Lord."

God exalted (lifted up) Jesus to the highest place in Heaven. Have we exalted Him to the highest place in our own life? Before we have any chance of communicating a message of truth with the world, we must have a message of truth residing in our heart. Have we truly accepted His forgiveness which only comes through faith, or are we still trying to earn our way, chasing after false messengers, and traveling down the broad road? Do we love Him with all our heart, soul, mind, and strength (Mark 12:30), or are we still just getting acquainted from a distance?

What about our place of worship? God has an important role for the local church and desires each of us to be in fellowship with other believers. But if our church does not lift up the name of Jesus Christ, it becomes little more than a social club leading an entire flock of lost sheep down the broad road of destruction. God forbid!

Let's exalt Jesus to the highest place in our life, in our home, and in our church. Let's love Him with all our heart and take active steps to draw closer to His presence. Let's show the world that eternal life is only through faith in the name which is above all other names - the name of Jesus.

WE HAVE BEEN SENT

In the last few messages, we have been encouraged to share the message of truth with whoever God places in our path. We saw the need to reach people where they are, "to the weak I became weak" (1 Corinthians 9:22), and the need to share an understandable message without self-righteous condemnation; but also, to share without compromise as we lift up the name of Jesus Christ.

The Word of God teaches there is only one way to Heaven: "I am the way and the truth and the life. No one comes to the Father except through Me" (John 14:6). Salvation is a gift of grace given to those who place their faith in the sacrifice of Jesus for the forgiveness of sin - there is no other way! And although relatively few will actually travel the narrow road that leads to life, the road is available to ALL who will come: "Everyone who calls on the name of the Lord will be saved" (Romans 10:13).

It's God's desire for everyone to call on His name; "not wanting anyone to perish, but everyone to come to repentance" (2 Peter 3:9), but not everyone will. Some have hardened their heart through continued rejection and willful disobedience, and now refuse to repent and receive the truth; others simply never hear the Good News.

Romans 10:14-15

"How, then, can they call on the one they have not believed in? And how can they believe in the one of whom they have not heard? And how can they hear without someone preaching to them? And how can they preach unless they are sent?"

Only God is able to draw someone near and lead them to repentance, and only the Holy Spirit can transform someone's heart into a "new creation" (2 Corinthians 5:17). But God has chosen to give His children the responsibility of sharing His message of forgiveness and truth with the world; "As You sent Me into the world, I have sent them into the world" (John 17:18).

In order for the message of Salvation to truly reach the world, we who know the truth must accept our commission to be "sent." We must be determined to share the gospel message whenever and wherever He directs; "Therefore go and make disciples of all nations" (Matthew 28:19). This may mean in another country, but it may also mean in our own backyard - or in our own family as we love them and demonstrate the true peace of Jesus.

Let's faithfully pick up the torch today. We have been given everything we need (2 Peter 1:3), we do not lack any Spiritual gift (1 Corinthians 1:7), and we have been declared ambassadors for Christ (2 Corinthians 5:20). The world is waiting to hear! Let's BOLDLY go forth with His Word, with an assurance that we have been sent!

GOD'S PLUMB LINE

A mos was a shepherd when God called him to preach to the northern kingdom of Israel. For more than one hundred and fifty years, the northern kingdom had worshipped by their own set of rules and even began to worship other gods. Amos was sent to reveal their sin and call the people to repentance. He warned they must return to God with all their heart or face certain judgment.

Amos 7:7-8

> *"This is what He showed me: The Lord was standing by a wall that had been built true to plumb, with a plumb line in His hand. Then the Lord said, 'Look, I am setting a plumb line among my people Israel; I will spare them no longer.'"*

A plumb line is simply a string with a weight on one end which will hang straight because of the unchanging pull of gravity. Plumb lines have been used for thousands of years as a guide. Building a wall seems relatively easy: stack one brick on top of another until the proper height and width is achieved. But without a reference line, it's nearly impossible to determine when the wall is straight. Without a true standard as a guide, our well-intended efforts produce a jagged mess which will soon crumble and fall.

God used a plumb line to show that the people of Israel had once been true, but now they were building their lives without a reference. God had established clear guidelines and preserved them within His Word. He was now bringing judgements according to His unchanging standard; "I will make justice the measuring line and righteousness the plumb line" (Isaiah 28:17).

The people did not listen to Amos' plea. They continued to live outside God's will and were guided by their own evil desires. God's judgement came thirty years after the end of Amos' ministry as He allowed the Assyrian army to march through the northern kingdom and bring complete destruction in 722 BC.

God is making the same call to us today. We cannot continue to build using the world's system of values as our reference. This is a standard in constant change, sinking deeper and deeper into the slimy pit. We may try to justify our actions by remaining slightly "above" the standard of the world; but as this standard continues to sink, we will follow it right down. This should NOT be our chosen path!!

Our lives need an unchanging reference to call us back when we stray. This reference must be the Word of God which calls us to a life of absolute pure devotion. When we build on the foundation of Christ and determine to love Him with ALL our heart, His Word ensures we will rise tall and not be found leaning to the left or right. Let's build a life which is true and does not waver - let's live by His Word and build according to God's plumb line.

THE LIVING WORD

In the message "God's Plumb Line" we were encouraged to build our lives upon the absolute and unwavering standard of God's Word. His Word is truth and holds the answer to every problem we will ever confront. If we search for answers and prayerfully reflect on the truth of God's Word - if we indeed consider His Word as absolute and unchanging, and apply it directly into our life - we will find the solutions have been available long before we were born.

Hebrews 4:12-13

"For the Word of God is living and active. Sharper than any double-edged sword, it penetrates even to dividing soul and spirit, joints and marrow; it judges the thoughts and attitudes of the heart. Nothing in all creation is hidden from God's sight. Everything is uncovered and laid bare before the eyes of Him to whom we must give account."

Without changing in content or meaning, the Word of God adapts to every situation. If we maintain the habit of reading and reflective study, we will find new insights in what appear to be the peeling back of multiple layers of understanding. But it is actually us who are being peeled back and laid bare by the ever present truths of His Word.

The passage, "Trust in the Lord with all your heart and lean not on your own understanding" (Proverbs 3:5), will have a much different meaning after we've obediently followed God for several years. Each time adversity strikes, we will find a deeper calling in the phrase "with ALL your heart." And though we walk with God for all the rest of our days, we may never fully appreciate the words; "God demonstrated His own love for us in this: While we were still sinners, Christ died for us" (Romans 5:8). How our lives would change if we could ever fully understand His love!

We do not truly "dig deeper" into the Word; rather, the Word digs deeper into us! Scriptural truths are not revealed until our hunger is so great that we are willing to place our life on the table and allow the sword of truth to cut deep inside. Do we really desire to know God, His Word, and His Spirit? Do we really want to understand the depth of God's love and the implications of His justice? Then be advised: even necessary and beneficial surgery can be painful. When our chest is opened, the condition of our heart is revealed; and that which is dark and displeasing must be cut away and burned.

But fear not! Our Heavenly Father is a skilled surgeon who can make our heart new and prepared to yield to His Spirit. The solution to our most complex problems is always found in His presence, and He has given His Word to show us how to draw near. Our lives are in need of some divine surgery today! Let's allow our heart to be cut by the truth - to be exposed and purified by the Living Word.

HE IS RISEN

On the night before He was crucified, Jesus, while in great anguish, showed the human side of His nature and asked if there was another way for God's plan to be accomplished; "My Father, if it is possible, may this cup be taken from Me" (Matthew 26:39a). Though He knew He would be physically, emotionally, and Spiritually tormented, nailed to a cross, and hung until dead, He gave His life into the hands of the Father; "Yet, not as I will, but as You will" (Matthew 26:39b). And as sure as Jesus knew God's plan was for Him to die, He also knew He would rise again; "And on the third day He will be raised to life" (Matthew 17:23).

On the third day after Jesus was crucified, Mary Magdalene and her friends saw the empty tomb and immediately ran to tell the disciples; "But they did not believe the women, because their words seemed to them like nonsense" (Luke 24:11). Even after Peter saw the empty tomb for himself, he was perplexed; "He went away, wondering to himself what had happened" (Luke 24:12).

The disciples had walked with Jesus and listened to Him teach about this day but they still did not understand. It wasn't until Jesus personally appeared to the disciples that the events began to make sense; "Then He opened their minds so they could understand the Scriptures" (Luke 24:45).

In an instant, everything fit into place. They finally understood how all the Old Testament scripture pointed to the coming of Jesus and how He would be sacrificed for the forgiveness of our sins. They saw the predictions of His death - and of His resurrection. They finally saw Him as much more than a good teacher, much more than even a mighty king. His resurrection meant He was the Savior, the one and only Son of God!

Romans 1:4

> *"And who through the Spirit of holiness was declared with power to be the Son of God by His resurrection from the dead: Jesus Christ our Lord."*

The resurrection was God's declaration to the world: "This is My Son!" The resurrection lets us know that "with God ALL things are possible" (Matthew 19:26), and it gives us the assurance that every one of His promises will come to pass; if Christ is truly risen, how can any trials of this world possibly lead to defeat?

True belief in the resurrection should fill us with awe and overwhelm us with a sense of peace and thankfulness. He died and rose again so we could live an abundant life and worship Him for all eternity. Let's place our faith in the sacrifice of Jesus for the forgiveness of our sins and live in the promise and power of His resurrection. Let's pray for our mind to be fully opened to His truth and for our life to be lived as though we KNOW He is risen!

PAID IN FULL

In the message "He is Risen" we were encouraged to live as though we know Jesus Christ is risen from the dead. Please don't skim past this encouragement because you think all Christians know this simple fact. The challenge is not in knowing the correct answer, but in living consistent with true knowledge in terms of thankfulness and perseverance - a life of hope and power. The following courtroom drama helps us understand the implications of a risen Lord.

The prosecution is aggressively presenting the case against us. There's a parade of witnesses and a multitude of accusations flung our way. Our head hangs low - we sadly realize that no objection can be raised - every charge against us is true. Our heart sinks as the prosecution confidently concludes his case; he has demanded the maximum penalty - death!

Our defense attorney has sat silently through the entire proceeding, but now He rises. His white robe glides across the floor as He moves between us and the Judge. Stretching out His arms, He reveals deep scars on both His wrists. He looks into the eyes of the Judge and says: "Father, while they were in the midst of their crimes, I died so they may live."

Without a moment of hesitation, the gavel sounds and the Judge declares: "Not Guilty!"

The verdict in God's courtroom is not dependent on the balance of good verses bad. There is no amount of good deeds and moral living which will ever cancel the charge against us; "For all have sinned and fall short of the glory of God" (Romans 3:23). And there is only one sentence we truly deserve; "For the wages of sin is death" (Romans 6:23).

But God has provided an Advocate, whom He has already approved by His resurrection, and who now stands ready to walk by our side; "We have one who speaks to the Father in our defense - Jesus Christ, the Righteous One" (1 John 2:1). This Advocate has only one requirement in order to present our case.

Romans 10:9

"If you confess with your mouth, 'Jesus is Lord,' and believe in your heart that God raised Him from the dead, you will be saved."

Believing in our heart means much more than simply knowing the story. It means a belief which pumps through every part of our body and gives us life! We need not live in fear - the verdict has already been determined; "there is now no condemnation for those who are in Christ Jesus" (Romans 8:1). We can "approach the throne of grace with confidence" (Hebrews 4:16), because we have already been declared not guilty. We are free to worship Him now and for all eternity because our debt has been paid in full!

DAYENU - JESUS IS ENOUGH

In the message "Paid in Full" we considered the sacrifice of Jesus as the payment for our sin. His sacrifice on the cross occurred during the Jewish Passover, a yearly time of celebration and remembrance ever since God led the nation of Israel out of Egypt.

The traditional Jewish Passover meal, or Seder, is designed to direct ones heart back to the praise and honor of God. One of the traditional Passover songs is called Dayenu, a Hebrew word meaning "it would have been enough." Each verse of this song recounts one of God's blessings and states if this was all God had done, it would have been enough - Dayenu!

If God had only led His people out of Egypt - Dayenu! (But He did more!). If He had only parted the sea - Dayenu! (But He did more!). If He had only fed them in the wilderness - Dayenu! (But He did more!). If He had only given His Holy Word - Dayenu! The Christian Jews add a final verse to this song which reminds them of how God saw a sinful people and yet loved them enough to give His Son.

Romans 5:6

"At just the right time, when we were still powerless, Christ died for the ungodly."

I'm often grieved by the lack of thankfulness in the world - for that matter, I'm often grieved by the lack of thankfulness in my own heart. I'm saddened by those who do not know God and fail to see His loving hand in all creation. I'm saddened by the Jewish people who have all the history of God's love, but, as a group, have lost their deep reverence and worship. Even in the midst of continual fighting, God is still calling the Jewish people back to a heart of true thanksgiving.

But mostly I'm saddened by Christians who place their trust in the sacrifice of Jesus, and yet live their life with an attitude which says: What have You done for me lately? God, You must not care about me because my job stinks, or my finances are a mess, or I'm unhappy in my relationship.

Can we even begin to understand how this must sound to God? When we were still powerless - when we were dead in our sin - God sent His Son to die so we could live! We live because of His love, yet we complain and grumble because of trivial fluff. Shame on us! Shame on me!!

Through faith in the sacrifice of Jesus, we are given the ability to stand and live in the presence of a Holy God - His death and resurrection is completely sufficient! (But He did even more!). He gave us His Spirit to strengthen us and guide us in His truth, and He gave us His peace which surpasses all human understanding. Let's remember the blessings we've already been given. God looked down and sent His One and Only Son - Dayenu! Jesus is Enough!!

HIS CONSUMING FIRE

Ice will turn to water at a temperature just above zero degrees centigrade. We might consider the water to be consumed as it turns to stream at one hundred degrees centigrade. Wood must be heated to a much higher temperature before it's consumed and metal must be heated even more. How much heat is required to finally consume the works of our flesh and burn away all selfishness and pride?

Hebrews 12:28-29

> *"Therefore, since we are receiving a kingdom that cannot be shaken, let us be thankful, and so worship God acceptably with reverence and awe, for our God is a consuming fire."*

When we begin to understand the Kingdom we've inherited through Christ, we dare not enter His sanctuary with anything but pure praise and worship. Whatever else we attempt to bring is born in our flesh with a spirit of pride. If we say, "Look at what I've brought You, my Lord!" He will simply burn it to ash. We might protest, "But God, look at all I've done for You!" and the heat will be turned up until all we hold is consumed.

Is our greatest ambition to impact the world for Christ? Is our motivation to be significant in the eyes of God or become a major player in the advancement of His Kingdom? Beware! Though these sound good and have the appearance of being pleasing to God, they are conceived in pride and will be consumed.

We truly can bring Him NOTHING of worth except a pure heart; "All our righteous acts are like filthy rags" (Isaiah 64:6). Our greatest desire (our ONLY desire) must be to praise and worship the King through all we think, say, and do. All our striving to be obedient and produce good works - all of our "Godly" motivation and ambition - must flow simply as a direct outpouring of our worship.

If we are still trying to conquer something for Christ, we have not yet fully submitted to His leading nor found complete rest in His strength. Jesus came with all knowledge and power, and yet He walked with absolute surrender and submission; "the world must learn that I love the Father and that I do exactly what My Father has commanded Me" (John 14:31).

This is a daily challenge, one of the more subtle battles between the Spirit and the flesh. While we must strive, we must also remember that God does not need anything we produce. True fruit which pleases our Heavenly Father comes only as we "remain in the vine" (John 15:4), and love Him with all our heart.

The same fire that will one day burn all our righteous acts can be used today to cleanse our heart. Let's come into His presence and worship with pure reverence and awe. Let's allow every selfish desire and every fiber of pride to be burned away in His consuming fire.

NEVER TRADE THE BLESSING

When Isaac was sixty years old, his wife Rebecca gave birth to twin sons. Esau was born first, followed immediately by Jacob; "with his hand grasping Esau's heal" (Genesis 25:26). Esau grew to be a skillful hunter while Jacob stayed more around the tents with his mother.

In the days of Esau and Jacob, the firstborn son was given a special honor called the birthright. The child having the birthright received a double portion of the family inheritance as well as the eventual privilege of family leadership. The birthright could be traded, but all future birthright blessings were then lost.

Genesis 25:29-32

"Once when Jacob was cooking some stew, Esau came in from the open country, famished. He said to Jacob, 'Quick, let me have some of that red stew! I'm famished!' Jacob replied, 'First sell me your birthright.' 'Look, I am about to die,' Esau said. 'What good is the birthright to me?'"

Esau was a young man who lived "in the moment" and traded his birthright for a bowl of stew. He placed much greater value on immediate gratification than on future blessings; and he exaggerated his immediate need in order to justify the future loss. The mighty hunter may have been hungry - maybe even VERY hungry - but he certainly was not about to die. His decision to let go of his birthright was based on the temporary needs he could see and feel; in turn, he lost the blessings which were greater and unseen.

Similar trades are being made today. When a child leaves home in rebellion, they trade an honoring relationship with their parents for perceived pleasures of immediate freedom. When a spouse pursues a relationship outside of marriage, they have traded a God-honoring union for perceived pleasures of the flesh. And when we fail to "wait upon the Lord" with decisions about a job, a move, a major purchase, or a relationship, we have allowed our impatience to trade away the blessing of walking in God's perfect will.

What bowl of stew are we trading for today? God has promised a blessing for those who believe in Jesus as Lord and Savior, for those who trust in Him for the forgiveness of sin and walk daily in His light. He has promised to set us free to live a life of true peace, purpose and contentment, and an eternal glory in His presence when we die. ALL worldly pleasures will one day fade away; "For what is seen is temporary, but what is unseen is eternal" (2 Corinthians 4:18). Let's devote our lives to worship and obediently follow wherever He leads. Let's keep our eyes on the eternal and NEVER trade the blessing.

STAY OFF THE ROOF

King David gave in to temptation with Bathsheba and then tried to cover up his sin with lies and murder. How could someone described by God as, "A man after My own heart" (Acts 13:22), make such a bad error in judgment? Sin is rarely the result of a single poor choice. Most often, the actual sin is caused by a long drift away from the presence of God and several specific decisions made outside His will.

2 Samuel 11:1

"In the spring, at the time when kings go off to war, David sent Joab out with the king's men and the whole Israelite army. They destroyed the Ammonites and besieged Rabbah. But David remained in Jerusalem."

David had become complacent about his duties as King. When the rest of his men were off at war, David stayed home with not much to do. He could have spent time drawing closer to God with prayer and study of the Word, but apparently David allowed himself to become quite restless.

2 Samuel 11:2

"One evening David got up from his bed and walked around on the roof of the

palace. From the roof he saw a woman bathing. The woman was very beautiful."

David walked out on the roof and (much to his surprise?) he saw a naked woman in a bathtub! David built this palace - he knew every detail of the architecture. David knew exactly where the bath houses were and knew the preferred times of bathing! "But each one is tempted when, by his own evil desire, he is dragged away and enticed. Then, after desire has conceived, it gives birth to sin" (James 1:14-15).

David's sin began long before he climbed into bed with Bathsheba. It began with letting down his guard of self-discipline and wandering from God, and it continued by entering an area of compromise.

We must all recognize our roof where we become susceptibility to temptation: "No temptation has seized you except what is common to man. And God is faithful; He will not let you be tempted beyond what you can bear. But when you are tempted, He will also provide a way out so that you can stand up under it" (1 Corinthians 10:13). Many times, our way out is simply to not visit the place where we know temptation resides - to not allow temptation to even germinate in our heart.

Is there a restlessness which is causing us to drift from God? Are we spending time and energy on activities, in places or conversations, we know are not honoring to God? Let's remain in His presences and ask God to open our eyes to the vulnerable areas of our life; let's commit to walk the path of purity and stay off the roof!

TWO BECOME ONE FLESH

In the message "Stay Off The Roof" we saw how seemingly innocent beginnings can have disastrous results when we entertain even the slightest area of temptation. This becomes even more critical when we marry; then, the result of temptation can cause great pain to the one given to us as a gift from God.

By the middle of the sixth day, God had created the sun, moon and stars; the land, sky, and water; the fish, birds, plants and animals - and when He looked at His creation, "God saw that it was good" (Genesis 1:25). But God's creation was not yet complete: "Then God said, 'let us make man in our image'" (Genesis 1:26), and out of the dust of the ground, God breathed life into man and put him in the Garden of Eden, "to work it and take care of it" (Genesis 2:15).

As God watched man go about his work, He saw that something was not right. Some have suggested that man looked a little sad - others have joked that man was making a big mess and kept wandering around, lost and confused. Whatever the cause, God looked at His latest creation and said:

Genesis 2:18

> *"It is not good for the man to be alone. I will make a helper suitable for him."*

Adam needed more than someone to help him with his chores, he needed someone to make him complete! So God formed woman, not from the ground, but from a rib taken from Adam's side; "This is now bone of my bones and flesh of my flesh" (Genesis 2:23).

If God gives us someone as a special gift to make us whole, they ought to be cherished and protected for a lifetime; "For this reason, a man will leave his father and mother and be united to his wife, and they will become one flesh" (Genesis 2:24). Like pieces of a puzzle that fit neatly together, a God-ordained marriage joins and completes by making two become one.

It's sad how quickly we forget these basic truths. We continue to place our individual desires ahead of the union created by God. We "toy" with temptations without regard to the potential devastation. The result is often a civil war with years of Spiritual bloodshed and an eventual ripping apart of what God has joined. We must stop this downward spiral before it even begins.

To the MANY single parents, I pray that God would give you encouragement and strength; I pray He would be the helper I know you desperately need. To those who are married or planning to marry, I pray we would now and forevermore see our spouse as a true gift from God given to make us whole. I pray we would forever thank Him for joining us together and commit to the protection of the union. I pray we would always remember that God provides our most suitable helper when the two become one flesh.

PASS THE TRUE BLESSING

When Jesus began His ministry on earth, He taught those who had an ear to hear, healed those who were sick, and fed those who were hungry. He also selected twelve Apostles and sent them "to the lost sheep of Israel" (Matthew 10:6) with instructions to preach, heal, and feed. As He was preparing them for the mission field, He gave a command to maintain a giving heart.

Matthew 10:8

"Freely you have received, freely give."

All we have is from the hand of God. There is nothing we can claim we have earned or deserve. If the material in this book has in any way blessed you and helped to draw you closer to God, I pray you would consider giving this book to someone else. Our Heavenly Father will continue to be glorified as we freely pass the blessing!

I included this message at the end of this book (as well as at the end of the other volumes in this series) as a way of encouraging people to share these books with others. These messages have only limited value if they are read once and put on the shelf.

But there is a much more general principle at work, and one much more important than the sharing of books. We have received from God the greatest gift of all, the gift of His Son. God gave His Son, free of charge to all who believe, as a full and complete sacrifice for the forgiveness of our sin. We may take the rest of our lives trying to comprehend the magnitude of this gift, but He has given us a way to spend all eternity with Him in Heaven. He has given us a ticket which instantly transports us from eternal death in Hell to eternal life in Heaven. Can anything compare? Yet the gift is free.

The gift is free and absolutely not for sale. We cannot purchase eternal life with all the money in the world or all the good deeds accomplished by every soul who ever walked the earth. The only way to receive the gift of eternal life is to humbly approach the Giver and believe.

But now that we have received such a wonderful gift we must give it away. We cannot keep the gift of Salvation on the shelf and hope to dust it off when we're finally called Home. We must share our faith - share our gift - with anyone, anywhere, and at any time that will express His love and glorify His name. Our ability to give away the gift reflects an understanding of its value and the free grace through which it was given. Let's share the free gift of Jesus with others today. Today, let's freely pass the true blessing.